The Cost of Health Insurance Administration

The Cost of Health Insurance Administration

An Economic Analysis

Roger D. Blair
University of Florida

Ronald J. Vogel
Social Security Administration

Lexington Books
D.C. Heath and Company
Lexington, Massachusetts
Toronto London

Library of Congress Cataloging in Publication Data

Blair, Roger D.
The cost of health insurance administration.

Bibliography: p.
Includes index.
1. Insurance, Health—United States—Costs. 2. Insurance companies—United States—Management—Costs. I. Vogel, Ronald J., joint author. II. Title.
HD7102.U4B59 338.4'3 75-21301
ISBN 0-669-00165-1

Published simultaneously in Canada.

Printed in the United States of America.

International Standard Book Number: 0-669-00165-1

Library of Congress Catalog Card Number: 75-21301

For Chau and Linda

Contents

List of Figures

List of Figures

List of Tables

Preface

A casual look at some data will confirm that the health insurance industry is a large and important industry in the United States. By 1971, about 90 percent of the population was covered by some form of health insurance.[1] If one includes Medicare, health *insurance* expenditures in 1971 amounted to $30.6 billion, or 2.9 percent of Gross National Product,[a] while total health expenditures in 1971 were $75.0 billion and represented 7.4 percent of GNP. By way of contrast, in that same year, factory sales of all automobile and parts were $46.7 billion and all cash receipts from farming, including government payments, were $53.1 billion.[2]

Table P-1 summarizes the health insurance situation in 1971. Blue Cross, Blue Shield, and medical society plans covered 42.4 percent of all persons under age sixty-five for hospital expenses and 40.3 percent of the same people for surgical expenses; commercial insurance companies and other plans covered the remaining insured population under age sixty-five. Medicare covered 10.9 percent of the insured population with hospital insurance and 11.4 percent of the insured population with surgical protection.[3] The commercial insurers, Blue Cross-Blue Shield, and Medicare paid 36 percent, 33 percent, and 31 percent, respectively, of all health insurance benefits in 1971. Thus, Medicare paid a much larger average claim per insuree than either the commercials or Blue Cross-Blue Shield. This result is to be expected, given the age and morbidity characteristics of the Medicare population. In that same year, $4.1 billion was spent on administering health insurance, with the commercial insurers spending 75 percent of that amount. The importance of administrative costs has not been lost on economists. Kenneth Arrow, has written

> The pure theory of insurance . . . omits one very important consideration: the costs of operating an insurance company. There are several types of operating costs, but one of the most important categories includes commissions and acquisition costs, selling costs in usual economic terminology. Not only does this mean that insurance policies must be sold for considerably more than their actuarial value, but it also means that there is a great differential among different types of insurance. It is very striking to observe that among health insurance policies of insurance companies . . . expenses of one sort or another constitute 51.6 percent of total premium income for individual policies and only 9.5 percent for group policies. . . . This striking differential would seem to imply *enormous economies of scale* in the provision of insurance, quite apart from the coverage of the risks themselves. Obviously, this provides a very strong argument for widespread plans, including, in particular, compulsory ones.[4]

[a]This figure includes $1.7 billion for disability income insurance and also includes health insurance administrative expenditures.

Table P-1
Health Insurance, 1971

I. Number of persons (in thousands):	
Commercial Insurers and Blue Cross-Blue Shield: (persons under 65)	
Hospital expense	168,513
Surgical expense	155,841
Regular medical expense	135,970
Major medical expense	78,516
Disability income:	
Short-term	58,850
Long-term	
Medicare:	
Hospital insurance	20,590
Supplementary medical insurance	20,012
II. Benefits paid (in millions):	
Insurance companies	$ 9,069
Hospital expense	4,391
Surgical, medical and dental expense	2,991
Disability income	1,687
Blue Cross, Blue Shield, and other hospital medical plans	8,711
Hospital expense	5,925
Surgical, medical and dental expense	2,786
Medicare[1]	7,478
Hospital insurance	5,443
Supplementary medical expense	2,035
Total	$25,258
III. Health insurance premiums (in millions)	
Insurance companies	$12,777
Group	9,170
Individual	3,607
Blue Cross, Blue Shield, and other hospital medical plans	9,996
Medicare[2]	7,875
Hospital insurance	5,592
Supplementary medical insurance	2,283
Total	$30,648
IV. Administrative Costs (in millions)	
Insurance companies	$3,000
Group	1,248
Individual	1,752
Blue Cross, Blue Shield, and other hospital medical plans	703
Medicare	397

Table P-1 (cont.)

IV. Administrative Costs (cont.)	
Hospital insurance	149
Supplementary medical insurance	248
Total	$4,100
V. Operating ratios	
Insurance companies	23.5%
Group	13.6
Individual	48.6
Blue Cross, Blue Shield, and other hospital medical plans	7.0
Medicare	5.0
Hospital insurance	2.7
Supplementary medical insurance	10.9%

Source: Health Insurance Institute, 1972-73 *Source Book of Health Insurance Data* (New York: Health Insurance Institute, 1973), p. 5. Marjorie Smith Mueller, "Private Health Insurance in 1971: Health Care Services, Enrollment, and Finances," *Social Security Bulletin*, February 1973, Table 13, p. 15. National Underwriter Company, *1972 Argus Chart of Health Insurance* (Cincinnati: National Underwriter, 1972), p. 112. Data on Medicare are from unpublished records of the Bureau of Health Insurance, Social Security Administration.

Notes:

1. Fiscal 1971.
2. Strictly speaking, Medicare has no premiums. The figures presented are administrative cost plus benefits paid which would be the equivalent, in an actuarial sense, of premiums paid.

It is clear that the health insurance industry[b] occupies a relatively large place in the economy. Furthermore, more than 14 percent of all monies collected from the public in order to provide health insurance protection are used to pay for administrative costs. In the past, there have been some sound studies of health insurance,[5] but there has never been an in-depth systematic study of the costs of administering health insurance. The absence of such a study gained particular importance due to the advent of Medicare. This importance emerged because of the role played by the existing firms as intermediaries and carriers. Given the present public policy debate about what form National Health Insurance should take, the lack of such a study becomes crucial. There have been many public statements by various persons and groups concerning the costs of administering health insurance. Many of these statements lack a factual basis or are misinterpretations of currently available statistical information. It is our hope that the present inquiry will provide a larger statistical base for the future debate on National Health Insurance. More fundamentally, however, we hope

[b]Even though Medicare is a program of the federal government, it is included as part of the health insurance industry because it fills a gap which long existed in coverage for the aged and because the major administrative work of the program is fulfilled by Blue Cross-Blue Shield and certain designated commercial companies.

that the analysis contained herein will provide a useful framework for viewing the costs of administering health insurance in all their complexity.

The central issue to which this study addresses itself is that of efficiency in the provision of health insurance. As is pointed out in the chapter entitled "The Concept of Cost," each of the present insuring entities—the commercial insurers, Blue Cross-Blue Shield, and Medicare—produces a different "output" in that they provide more than just health insurance. In other words, they perform different functions, the costs of which are not separately identifiable. Thus, direct comparisons of relative efficiency cannot be made due to the nonexistence of functional cost data. Nevertheless, estimation of cost functions, based upon economic theory, allows one to draw inferences about efficiency. The major portion of this study is concentrated upon the estimation of these cost functions and upon the inferences about efficiency which flow from those estimates.

Chapter 1, which contains an abstract discussion of the concept of cost, addresses itself to the problem of how one should view costs and discusses the difficulties in comparing the administrative costs of health insurance across the three main health insurers: the commercial insurers, Blue Cross-Blue Shield, and the Medicare program. The empirical analyses of Chapters 2, 3, and 4 have significance directly in proportion to the richness of the data sources available. The least amount of data was obtainable for the commercial insurers and the largest amount of statistical data was available for Medicare. Accordingly, in Chapter 2 we statistically analyze the administrative costs of the commercial insurance companies. In Chapter 3, we analyze the operating cost structure of the Blue Cross-Blue Shield plans and in Chapter 4 we examine the administrative cost components of Medicare. Chapter 5 contains our summary and conclusions.

Notes

1. Majorie Smith Mueller, "Private Health Insurance in 1971: Health Care Services, Enrollment, and Finances," *Social Security Bulletin*, February 1973, p. 11.

2. U.S. Dept. of Commerce, *Survey of Current Business*, December 1972.

3. Health Insurance Institute, 1972-73, *Source Book of Health Insurance* (New York: Health Insurance Institute, 1973), p. 5.

4. Kenneth J. Arrow, "Uncertainty and the Welfare Economics of Medical Care," *American Economic Review* 53, 5 (December 1963):963, emphasis added. Reprinted with permission.

5. See Duncan M. MacIntyre, *Voluntary Health Insurance and Rate Making* (Ithaca: Cornell University Press, 1962); Roy J. Hensley, *Competition, Regulation and the Public Interest in Nonlife Insurance* (Berkeley: University of California Press, 1962).

Acknowledgments

Many people have helped us greatly in the course of this study. We would be sadly remiss if we were to fail to thank them publicly and acknowledge their contributions. Stuart H. Altman, as Deputy Assistant Secretary for Planning and Evaluation/Health, DHEW, first interested us in the topic and provided encouragement. We would also like to thank David Robbins of the Health Insurance Association of America, Theodore Collum of the Nationwide Insurance Company, Joseph Woosley, Bernard Tresnowski, and Merrit Jacoby of Blue Cross, and George David of Blue Shield for assistance in obtaining data and counsel in the avoidance of pitfalls. There is an entire legion of people within the Social Security Administration who aided us in obtaining data, offered advice, and secured resources for our use. We especially would like to mention the names of Dorothy Rice, Howard West, Douglas Wilson, Charles Fisher, and Saul Waldman.

The entire manuscript was read by Bernard Friedman, Paul Ginsburg, John Hambor, Ronald Hoffman, William Sobaski, Mark Pauly, and Charles Phelps. We received comments on Chapter 2 from Ralph Berry, Hendrick Houthakker, Jerry Jackson, Jan Kmenta, Bridger Mitchell, and Frank Sloan. Various drafts of Chapter 3 were read by Mary Lou Larmore, Bridger Mitchell, and Roger Noll. Karen Davis and a number of the members of the staff of the Office of Research and Statistics reviewed Chapter 4. Finally, Daniel Hammermesh and Jan Kmenta provided useful econometric advice.

While any credit must be shared with all these people, the authors naturally assume full responsibility for what follows.

The Cost of Health Insurance Administration

1 The Concept of Cost

It is well known that the cost functions of a firm depend upon its production function and the prices it must pay for inputs.[1] We may assume that the firm produces its output according to the twice-differentiable production function

$$Q = f(x_1, x_2, \ldots, x_n), \tag{1.1}$$

where x_i denotes the quantity of the ith input. If the firm is a competitor in the factor markets, we can denote the price of the ith input as p_i. This means that the price paid by the firm for any input is independent of the quantity of the input purchased. Thus, for any input combination selected by the firm, the total cost of the combination is given by

$$C = \sum_{i=1}^{n} p_i x_i. \tag{1.2}$$

The *optimal* combination of inputs to minimize the cost of a predetermined quantity of output can be formulated as a Lagrangean constrained optimization problem:

$$L = \sum_{i=1}^{n} p_i x_i - \lambda [f(x_1, x_2 \ldots, x_n) - \bar{Q}], \tag{1.3}$$

where $\bar{Q}$ is the predetermined output level and λ is the (undetermined) Lagrange multiplier.

The first-order conditions for a constrained minimum require that all the first partial derivatives of Equation (1.3) vanish. Thus, we obtain first-order conditions

$$\frac{\partial L}{\partial x_i} = p_i - \lambda f_i = 0 \qquad (i = 1, 2, \ldots, n) \tag{1.4a}$$

$$\frac{\partial L}{\partial \lambda} = f(x_1, \ldots, x_n) - \bar{Q} = 0, \tag{1.4b}$$

where f_i is defined as $\partial f / \partial x_i$.

The condition (1.4b) merely insures that the quantity of inputs is sufficient to produce the predetermined output. In other words, satisfaction of (1.4b) means that the output constraint has been met. Equations (1.4a) yield the familiar conditions

$$\frac{f_i}{f_j} = \frac{p_i}{p_j} \qquad (i, j = 1, 2, \ldots, n) \qquad (1.5)$$

after eliminating λ. More specifically, cost minimization requires the equality of the marginal rate of technical substitution between any two inputs and the ratio of their respective prices. Alternatively, we may write

$$\frac{f_1}{p_1} = \frac{f_2}{p_2} = \ldots = \frac{f_n}{p_n}, \qquad (1.6)$$

which is sufficient to define the firm's expansion path.

The expansion path is defined in input space. If we map the expansion path from input space to the cost-output space, we obtain the total cost curve, $C(Q)$. The usual cost curves, *viz.*, the average and marginal cost curves, are obtained directly from the total cost curve according to the following definitions:

$$\text{Marginal cost} \equiv dC(Q)/dQ$$

and

$$\text{Average cost} \equiv C(Q)/Q.$$

The short-run cost curves are determined by holding one or more of the inputs fixed. As the quantity of the fixed input(s) is varied, the short-run average cost curve changes. The shape of the long-run average cost curve, which is the envelope of the short-run average cost curves, is determined by the specification of the production function.

Figure 1-1 depicts the behavior of the LAC curve under three different types of conditions. In panel (a), economies of scale are present. This means that as the firm expands output it becomes more efficient and per unit costs of output falls. In panel (b), the firm's LAC curve is U-shaped, which means that economies of scale are present initially, but that diseconomies of scale set in and the LAC curve will begin to rise as output continues to expand. In panel (c), the firm faces diseconomies of scale, i.e., the firm becomes less efficient as output expands and LAC are increasing everywhere.

The best way to determine the firm's cost curves is to start with the production function. In practice, however, the production function is empiri-

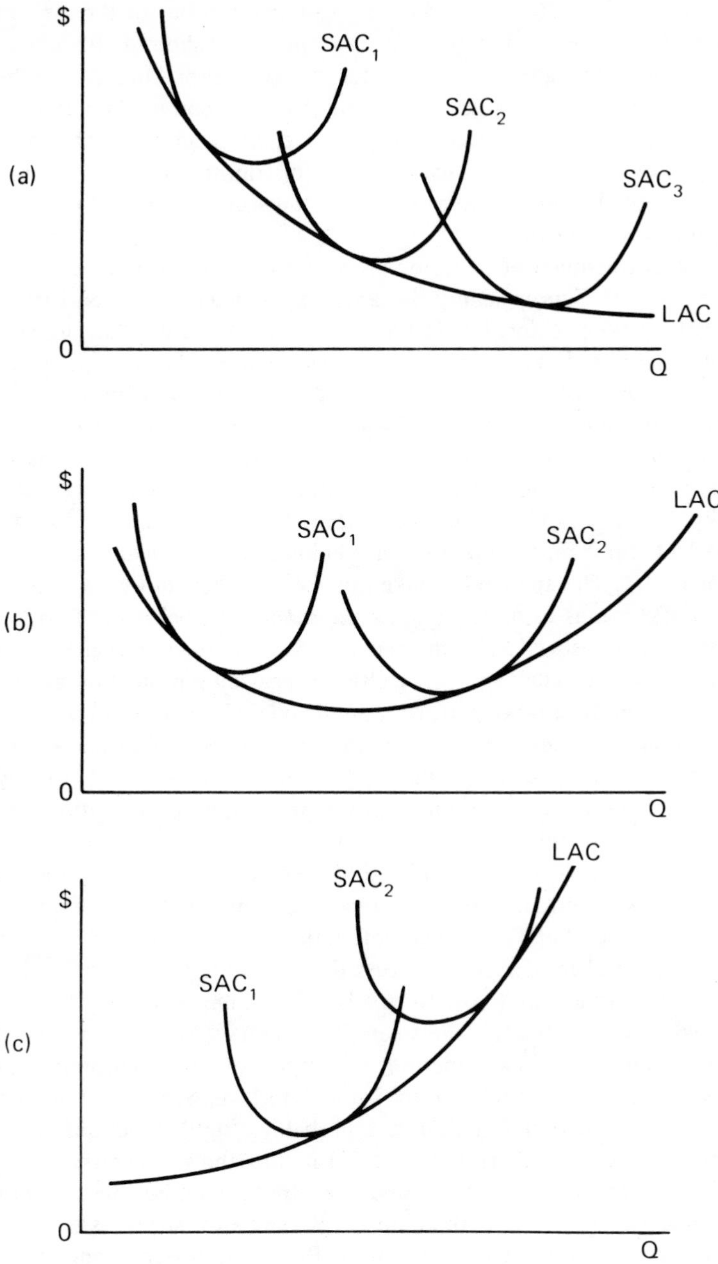

Figure 1-1. Behavior of LAC Curve Under Three Different Types of Conditions

cally elusive. An alternative procedure is to specify a form for the average cost function and estimate it directly. We have, in fact, followed this alternative. More specifically, we have not examined a particular firm, but have employed a cross-sectional analysis. In other words, we do not observe a single firm as it adjusts its inputs over time. Instead, we observe the entire array of firms in the industry at a moment in time. Given the size distribution of the existing firms, we can use these observations to estimate the long-run average cost curve for the implicit production function.

In the usual treatment of costs and production, the discussion centers around a tangible output. Conceptually, the analysis immediately generalizes to the output of the service sector, but in a very real sense some difficult problems are overlooked. With a few notable exceptions, economists have neglected the service sector. One consequence of this neglect is that output measures for the service industries are sadly lacking. This is just as true of the health insurance industry as of any other service industry. In most empirical studies of the insurance industry, the unit of output is defined to be premium volume. More specifically, it is taken to be premiums written. At least one empirical study[2] has found the LAC curve for the life insurance industry to be similar to that of panel (a) in Figure 1-1. The approaches taken in these studies, however, may not be the most useful means of understanding the nature and behavior of costs in the health insurance industry. Health insurance provides protection against a random event—the costs associated with ill health. In providing protection against this random event, the firm must perform a multitude of functions. The firm must sell the insurance policies, process applications, process policies, maintain the policies, process claims, review claims, pay the claims, and so on. Clearly, the consumer buys more than a simple contingency claim against future losses of wealth. The firm, of course, incurs costs in fulfilling its various functions and these costs may be only indirectly related to premium volume. Since the costs of performing these functions may be more a function of the type of application submitted, the type of application accepted, the number and kinds of policies in force, and the number of claims processed, one must be concerned about an appropriate output measure to use for the health insurance industry.[3]

Recognizing the distinction between fixed and variable costs, one might distribute the various costs as functions of output for a health insurance firm in the following schematic outline (see Table 1-1).[4] As Schuchardt points out, many of the variable cost functions are probably "step" functions. The costs associated with items (2), (3), (4), and (5) in the above schematic are apt to increase in discrete increments because the inputs required must be hired in discrete units. For example, as the number of claims to be processed increases, additional personnel will have to be hired. But additions are made in discrete units. This means that the cost function will jump when the number of claims passes each threshold that requires an additional claims processor. Tables 1-2 and 1-3 present hypothetical data that indicate how the cost-output relationship

Table 1-1
Costs as Functions of Output for a Health Insurance Firm

Variable	Output
(1) Commissions, premium taxes, boards and bureau fees	Premium written
(2) Applications processing	Applications processed (weighted)
(3) Policy processing	Policies processed (weighted)
(4) Policy maintenance	Number of policies (weighted)
(5) Claims processing	Number of claims processed (weighted)
Fixed	
(1) Salaried personnel	
(2) Buildings and equipment	Fixed costs are incurred to produce all of the forms of output listed above
(3) Property taxes and all other fixed monetary commitments such as association memberships, advertising	

Source: Schuchardt, Robert A., *Managerial Accounting in the Property and Casualty Business*, (Cincinnati: The National Underwriter Company, 1969)© 1969 by the National Underwriter Company. Reprinted with permission.

might appear for a typical health-insuring firm. These data are plotted in Figures 1-2 and 1-3. The general shapes of the functions are consistent with the empirical findings for life insurance companies.[5]

The preceding example shows that as a health insurance firm grows larger its average administrative expenses will decline. As long as the firm remains a pure competitor in its purchase of inputs, this relationship holds irrespective of input prices. The impact of varying input prices will be to shift the entire average cost functions up or down, but the general shape remains unchanged.

There are other reasons for suspecting that the shape of the long-run average cost function will be downward sloping as the firm grows larger. In a small-scale operation, it is uneconomical to use sophisticated electronic data processing equipment. As the firm's clientele increases, EDP equipment may be added to replace many of the manual operations involved and fewer clerks are needed for applications and policy processing, policy maintenance and claims processing. These functions are precisely those which contribute to the step-variable costs mentioned above. EDP equipment, on the other hand, demands a large initial outlay and comes in fairly large lumpy units, making fixed costs a relatively more important percentage of total costs than when only manual labor was used. It can easily be shown that as fixed costs become a larger percentage of total costs, the short-run average cost function of the firm will fall at a more rapid rate when output grows.[a] Thus, the substitution of EDP equipment for manual labor should result in substantial economies to the firm and cause the short-run average cost function to be downward sloping. For the same reasons, we would also expect the short-run average cost function of the entire industry to be downward sloping, with larger firms using EDP to have lower costs than smaller firms with limited EDP capabilities. On an a priori basis, then, one would expect larger firms to have lower average administrative costs than smaller firms. In the absence of regulation on rates, this gives the larger firms a competitive advantage and would tend to dictate higher concentration in the industry over time. The logical implication of this last statement is that the insurance industry might be a natural monopoly. The empirical section of this study, however, will show that the long-run average cost function of the firm and the industry flattens out at some point. Furthermore, the existence of intense product differentiation does not always give the firm with the lowest costs the advantage in the competition to sell health insurance.

---

[a]The demonstration of this is straightforward. We know that

$$ATC = AVC + AFC.$$

The slope of ATC is given by

$$\frac{d\,ATC}{dQ} = \frac{d\,AVC}{dQ} + \frac{d\,AFC}{dQ}$$

and the rate of change of the slope of ATC is given by

$$\frac{d^2ATC}{dQ^2} = \frac{d^2AVC}{dQ^2} + \frac{d^2AFC}{dQ^2}$$

Suppose that the only difference between two cost functions is the fixed cost component. Then the terms involving AVC will be unchanged. Since the average fixed cost curve is a rectangular hyperbola, it is of the form

$$AFC = \frac{TFC}{Q}$$

Examine the difference between $\frac{d^2AFC}{dQ^2}$

when $TFC = 100$ and $TFC = 200$. For $TFC = 100$, $\frac{d^2AFC}{dQ^2} = \frac{200}{Q^3}$. In contrast for $TFC =$ 200, $\frac{d^2AFC}{dQ^2} = \frac{400}{Q^3}$

Thus, for any value of Q, the rate of change of the slope of ATC is greater, the greater are the initial fixed costs.

Table 1-2
Hypothetical Example of Total Fixed and Variable Costs in a Health Insurance Firm

[In millions]

Premium volume	Fixed costs (1)	Step variable costs (2)	Pure variable costs (3)	(2)+(3) (4)	Total costs (1)+(4)
$110	$10	$20	$22	$42	$52
100	10	20	20	40	50
90	10	15	18	33	43
80	10	15	16	31	41
70	10	15	14	29	39
60	10	10	12	22	32
50	10	10	10	20	30
40	10	10	8	18	28
30	10	5	6	11	21
20	10	5	4	9	19
10	10	5	2	7	17

Table 1-3
Average Fixed Costs, Average Variable Costs, Average Costs and Marginal Costs for Hypothetical Firm Computed from Table 1-1

Volume (in millions)	AFC (1)	AVC (2)	AC (1)+(2)	MC
$110	$.09	$.38	$.45	$.20
100	.10	.40	.50	.70
90	.11	.37	.48	.20
80	.13	.39	.51	.20
70	.14	.41	.56	.70
60	.17	.37	.53	.20
50	.20	.40	.60	.20
40	.25	.45	.70	.70
30	.33	.37	.70	.20
20	.50	.45	.95	.20
10	1.00	.70	1.70	0.00

The major difficulty with the formulation of this theoretical analysis is the assumption of a homogeneous output for all firms. While this assumption is convenient theoretically and expositionally, it raises serious questions about the relevance of the model in analyzing the real world heatlh insurance industry. We will now consider some of the problems involved in comparing Medicare, Blue Cross-Blue Shield, and the commercial insurers.

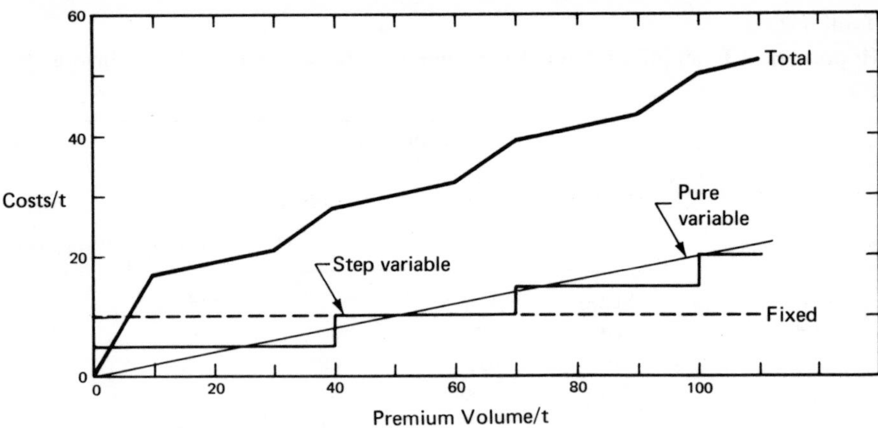

Figure 1-2. Costs as a Function of Premium Volume, Hypothetical Firm

Problems with Presently Used Concepts of Cost

Although the payment of claims is the major function performed by health insurance organizations, it is not the sole function. Administrative costs are incurred in providing all the services offered by the health insurer. For example, the individual consumer may be interested in more than comparable coverage when considering various insurance policies. One insurance firm may offer better services than another. If a consumer knows that he can obtain service at any hour of the day or night from one firm, he may be willing to pay more for that insurance policy because he is also buying the service differential. In addition, an individual might purchase health insurance at a higher price from a particular firm because the firm espouses and supports causes in which that individual believes, such as community service or research. In this instance, the consumer is purchasing health insurance, but he is also investing in his community or engaging in philanthropy.

Given the diverse activities, services, and interests of health insuring organizations in the United States, an investigation of the relative efficiencies of health insurers would need to give empirical content to a formulation such as the following:

$$A = 1 - \frac{c + s + r}{P} \tag{1.7}$$

In this formulation, c represents claims payments (the pure insurance component), s denotes the monetary costs of providing the services that an individual

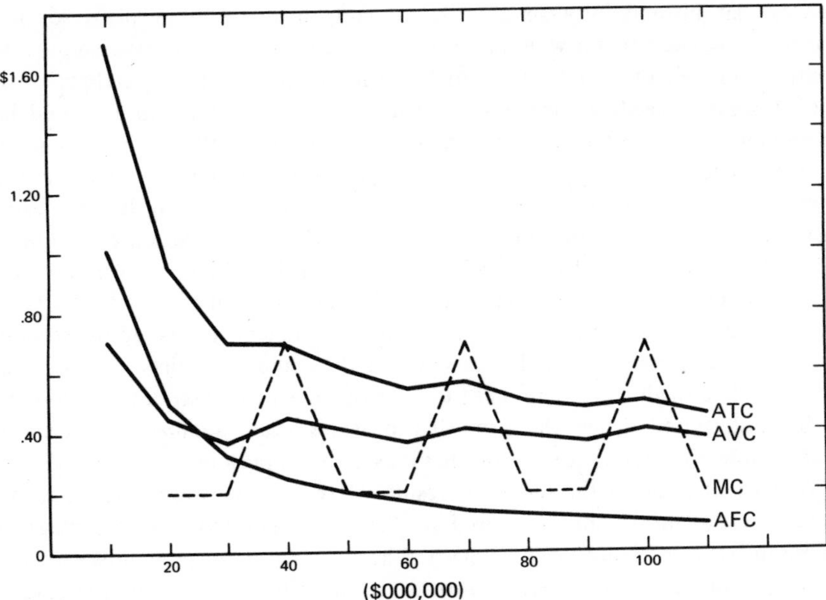

Figure 1-3. Average and Marginal Costs as a Function of Premium Volume, Hypothetical Firm

buys along with his insurance, *r* denotes the return on invested capital necessary[b] to keep the firm's resources in the industry, and *P* denotes premiums paid. Then *A* becomes the proportion of total premiums paid that covers the administrative costs of the pure health insurance. Since this expression isolates the proportion devoted to administering the pure insurance function, it is the parameter that is relevant for purposes of comparability. This expression explicitly factors out the value of *s* for the different health insurance organizations. It is imperative that this be done to hold constant all of the diverse functions which are performed, so that attention can be focused solely upon how much it costs the various organizations to administer their health insurance function.

In practice, however, the task of isolating *s* for each insuring organization and assigning it a monetary value poses many difficulties of a concentual and empirical nature. For example, Medicare produces health insurance for the aged; *s* in Medicare consists of provider certification, civil rights enforcement, and preventive measures against medical cost inflation. Blue Cross-Blue Shield attempts community rating and, thus, performs a certain amount of income redistribution from the well to the sick, it further attempts to monitor cost increases on the part of providers, which is an investment for policyholders.

[b]In fact, the insurance firm need not earn a profit on the business of insuring against risks because it makes a profit on its investment activities.

Commercial insurers provide a great amount of diversity in plans so that consumers might enjoy a wide range of choice; commercial insurers also provide multiple lines of insurance, which makes it more convenient to purchase all of one's insurance needs at one point. Each of these diverse functions could be considered to be contained in s because to a greater or lesser degree, they are services which are purchased *together with* health insurance. Isolating the monetary values of these various functions is no mean feat given the vagaries of cost accounting procedures and the somewhat arbitrary allocation of overhead items. To the extent that one fails to properly cost these functions for inclusion in Equation (1.7), a bias is introduced into the value of A. If the costs of services are overstated, then the firm appears more efficient in its administrative function. Conversely, if such costs are understated, the firm appears less efficient. One might speculate that the costs of these diverse services would tend to be understated. Then the firm that provides fewer auxiliary services will appear more efficient—a conclusion that may well be spurious.

As an indication of the operating results of the commercial insurance firms, the cost ratios most commonly used are "expenses incurred as a percentage of premiums written"[c] and "claims incurred as a percentage of premiums earned." These two ratios are combined to provide an indication of the operating results of the commercial companies.[6] The rationale for expressing expenses incurred as a percentage of premiums written rather than premiums earned is that commissions and other acquisition and field supervision costs are dependent primarily upon *writing* the policies.[7] In contrast, claims expenses are incurred as premiums are being earned.

Table 1-4 gives the operating results of the fifty largest commercial health insurers in 1971. The reader will note that, in most cases, the combined ratios exceed 100 percent, which indicates that the insurers incurred "underwriting losses," i.e., claims incurred plus operating expenses exceed premiums earned. This does not necessarily mean that the companies did not make a profit on their health insurance business because investment income is not included and the "claims incurred" column may be arbitrarily changed depending upon adjustment of incurred loss reserves.[d]

For purposes of comparability, the expenses incurred in the delivery of health

[c]A distinction is made between "premiums written" and "premiums earned" because commercial insurance premiums are generally paid on an annual basis by the consumer. Premiums are "earned" as the policy provides protection over time. Thus, if a consumer pays $300 for a health insurance policy on January 1, his insurance company has premiums written of $300 and premiums earned of $0. By July 1, premiums written would still be $300 and premiums earned would be $150.

[d]Premiums earned and claims incurred are kept on an accrual basis by the companies. Because there is no way of precisely knowing the amount of claims actually incurred until they are submitted for payment, the companies estimate the amount of claims incurred and place them in an incurred loss reserve. The funds contained in the incurred loss reserve are included in the "claims incurred" column. In the past ten years, the incurred loss reserve has increased as a percent of premiums earned.

insurance must be expressed in relation to some other variable common to the commercial insurers, Blue Cross-Blue Shield, and Medicare. The usual practice is to use premiums earned (or earned subscription income in the case of the Blues) as the base when comparing the performance of commercial insurers or the Blues. With Medicare, however, there are no comparable premium payments.[e] Because Medicare is a government program, it should theoretically always break even, with revenues being equal to the sum of operating costs and claims. Thus, one could argue that a Medicare base comparable to premiums earned could be the operating costs plus claims. Such a formulation, however, will overstate Medicare's administrative expenses on a ratio basis, comparable to those ratios contained in Table 1-4, because premiums earned for the Blues and the commercials contain slack for claims, plus additions to reserves plus a "profit." This is a severe handicap of this measure because one surely would not want to conclude that Medicare was less efficient simply because no "profit" was earned or because no slack were built into the base in order to build up reserves.[f]

The result of the structural differences in the health insurance organizations is that there exists no appropriate measure for purposes of comparison. If premiums earned are used as a base, there is the problem that Medicare does not have premiums. A substitute for premiums earned for Medicare might be claims plus administrative costs. This measure, however, will tend to overstate Medicare's administrative costs relative to those of the commercials and the Blues. If claims only are used as the base for all three insuring organizations, those organizations which provide the broadest range of services, besides insurance, will tend to have the cost of administering the insurance function overstated.

Further difficulties arise because all of the administrative costs are not explicit, i.e., are not compensated monetarily. As an illustration, all other things being equal, a country where all wives engage in market work will have a larger Gross National Product than a country where all wives work in their homes. Although wives in both countries might expend the same amount of energy in their respective forms of work, wives in the market country receive monetary remuneration, which enters into the definition of GNP, whereas those who work in the home receive no monetary remuneration. The work in the home is not counted as part of the national output, given the way GNP is defined. Clearly, a comparison of the two GNP's would be misleading because there would not be an accurate measure of the *real* amount of output in a country where all wives work in the home. In measuring the cost of delivering health insurance, a similar pitfall must be avoided. The cost of delivering health insurance includes not only the monetary administrative costs borne by the provider of the insurance but

[e]It is true that the Medicare recipient does pay a premium under Part B of the program but his premium in no way reflects the actuarial expectation of his group's loss, because Medicare is subsidized intergenerationally through the general fund.

[f]This is not to say that Medicare has no reserves. In fact, Medicare reserves number in the billions, but the reserves do not require slack in the base.

Table 1-4
Operating Experience, 50 Largest Commercial Health Insurers, 1971

	Premiums written (in thousands)	Premiums earned (in thousands)	Claims incurred (in thousands)	Expenses incurred (in thousands)	Claims incurred to premiums written	Expenses incurred to premiums written	Combined (5)+(6)
Aetna Life and Casualty	1,121,654	1,072,317	977,336	115,709	91.1	10.3	101.4
Travelers	1,026,270	986,336	889,346	109,879	90.2	10.7	100.9
Metropolitan Life	894,496	865,385	768,584	138,449	88.8	15.5	104.3
Prudential	861,617	856,329	726,032	141,117	84.8	16.4	101.2
Equitable Society	620,671	613,415	560,491	77,528	91.4	12.5	103.9
Connecticut General Life	578,009	562,479	515,444	66,983	91.6	11.6	103.2
Mutual of Omaha	498,811	492,527	354,288	129,945	71.9	26.1	98.0
CNA/Insurance	460,950	458,413	352,727	110,351	76.9	23.9	100.8
John Hancock Mutual Life	338,237	338,215	298,660	49,775	88.3	14.7	103.0
Provident L and A, Tenn.	288,847	289,610	255,220	35,657	88.1	12.3	100.4
Bankers Life and Casualty	253,352	236,982	138,316	85,693	58.4	33.8	92.2
Occidental Life, California	249,747	255,939	239,401	27,453	93.5	11.0	104.5
New York Life	213,956	208,890	181,879	45,940	87.1	21.5	108.6
Lincoln National Life	170,331	168,901	155,353	22,497	92.0	13.2	105.2
Combined Insurance Co.	164,886	159,972	66,933	70,913	41.8	43.0	84.8
The Union Labor Life	160,604	160,213	149,709	11,182	93.4	7.0	100.4
Bankers Life Company	145,108	144,362	125,555	21,523	87.0	14.8	101.8
Washington National	144,517	142,881	107,826	38,940	75.5	26.9	102.4
Union Mutual Life, Me.	119,713	118,396	101,745	20,187	85.9	16.9	102.8
Republic National Life	114,528	114,448	103,680	12,873	90.6	11.2	101.8
Pacific Mutual Life	114,107	113,916	100,808	15,452	88.5	13.5	102.0
Massachusetts Mutual Life	96,310	95,087	80,948	14,072	85.1	14.6	99.7
Hartford Life	95,909	88,823	69,985	22,088	78.8	23.0	101.8

General American Life	94,112	94,025	82,335	11,922	87.6	12.8	100.4
Allstate	90,923	79,432	69,855	11,487	87.9	12.6	100.5
Continental Insurance	90,388	92,251	55,686	32,338	60.4	35.8	96.2
United Insurance, Illinois	86,845	83,838	39,035	41,259	46.6	47.5	94.1
Mutual of New York	79,949	77,231	62,421	22,067	80.8	27.6	108.4
Great-West Life	74,071	73,015	64,407	12,097	88.2	16.3	104.5
Liberty Mutual	73,535	75,450	65,888	8,198	87.3	11.1	98.4
Paul Revere Life	71,267	68,142	44,247	25,522	64.9	35.8	100.7
Fireman's Fund American Life	65,137	65,700	65,904	14,867	100.3	22.8	123.1
Pilot Life	59,383	59,455	52,748	9,375	88.7	15.8	104.5
Reserve Life, Texas	58,965	56,552	30,753	24,891	54.4	42.2	96.6
Physicians Mutual	57,743	56,016	36,850	19,310	65.8	33.4	99.2
Benefit Trust Life	54,670	54,338	47,783	10,330	87.9	18.9	106.8
National Life and Accident	52,761	50,283	21,671	27,327	43.1	51.8	94.9
Independent Life and Accident	50,004	49,678	19,946	21,128	40.2	42.3	82.5
California Western States	49,842	50,200	45,136	7,045	89.9	14.1	104.0
Employers Life, Wausaw	49,605	49,618	45,144	6,421	91.6	12.9	104.5
Guardian Life, New York	48,790	46,968	35,457	14,382	75.5	29.5	105.0
Confederation Life	47,911	47,930	40,249	7,603	84.0	15.9	99.9
Colonial Penn Life	47,057	48,247	30,536	7,804	63.3	16.6	79.9
Business Men's Assurance	46,127	45,705	35,820	10,857	78.4	23.5	101.9
Monarch Life	44,784	41,606	26,889	14,113	64.6	31.5	96.1
American National	43,160	44,881	31,287	20,902	69.7	48.4	118.1
Pennsylvania Life, California	42,618	39,611	18,992	16,243	47.9	38.1	86.0
Nationwide	38,982	38,418	31,076	8,234	80.9	21.1	102.0
American Republic, La.	38,697	37,213	23,146	15,775	62.2	40.8	103.0
National Casualty	37,756	37,155	26,278	12,899	70.7	34.2	104.9

Source: The National Underwriter Company, *1972 Argus Chart of Health Insurance* (Cincinnati: The National Underwriter Company, 1972).

also those real (but nonpecuniary) costs incurred by individuals who must fill out claim forms and perform other non-reimbursed tasks. Furthermore, it is necessary to make a distinction between costs to the individual policyholder and costs to third parties. For example, the commercial insurers underwrite an unspecified number of group health insurance contracts in which all (or varying amount) of the administrative work is done by the insuree's employer. The costs to the employer of administering these insurance plans are unavailable. Also, physicians, hospitals, and patients may be legitimately viewed as performing part of the administrative work of health insurance. There are no reliable estimates of the amounts of time that all of these individuals spend on claims forms but it must be considerable.[8] This is only important if there are differences in the size of these costs among groups of insurers. There is some evidence, however, that this is the case because of the reporting (or filing) requirements of the different firms.

In a period of rising prices, the comparison of ratios alone conceals trade-offs, which may be made within an insuring organization. Breaking even or making a profit is a function of premiums collected, claims paid, and administrative costs. If claims costs are high and rise at high rates and the demand for insurance is relatively inelastic, premium rates may be raised and administrative costs kept constant. If, on the other hand, the insuring organization makes an effort to monitor claims, resist inflation, and control the quality of services which its insurees receive, it may not have to raise premium rates. Its administrative costs, however, will probably increase. To frame this point in an analytically more precise form, consider the relationship in Equation (1.8):

$$B = P - (A + C) \tag{1.8}$$

where B is the breakeven point, or a targeted level of profit, P is premium volume, A is administrative costs, and C is claims costs. Simple arithmetic demands that the ratios considered earlier will vary widely, depending upon which variables the differing insuring organizations used to achieve B. One insurer may be lax on claims review. Consequently, his C may be relatively high while A may be lower because he uses less staff. Another insurer may have a lower C but A may be higher because of his extensive use of claims examiners. A third insurer may be able to raise P to compensate for increases in A or C. The insurees of all three insurers may be receiving the same amount of real medical care and real health insurance, but the above-mentioned ratios will differ.

Finally, comparisons of ratios are difficult because the relative size of administrative costs are a function of a number of variables, which may differ from organization to organization. Included among those factors which may differ are

1. the age-sex composition of the clientele, which would lead to a different size of the average claim, a different distribution of claims by size of claims, and a different frequency of claim per insuree;

2. definition of what is a claim;
3. benefit structures;
4. manners of reimbursing providers;
5. the size of the insurer;
6. the payment or non-payment of taxes; and
7. the size of selling (or enrollment) costs.

In sum, economic theory would lead us to posit an average cost function of the following form:

$$AC = f(\text{SERVICES, SIZE, PMIX, AGE, SEX, TAXES, SALES, WORK, QUALITY})$$

where AC could be defined in a number of ways. One way could be administrative costs as a percentage of premiums written; another way could be administrative costs per insuree.

For the independent variables, SERVICES would be an index of the services other than the pure health insurance provided and, SIZE would be a variable measuring the size of the insurer and could be defined as a premium volume or number of insurees. We would expect a positive relation between SERVICES and AC and an inverse relation between SIZE and AC. Because insurers in the United States offer such a large array of policies, PMIX would be a product mix variable or a number of product mix variables. One measure of product mix is the amount of group insurance offered as a percentage of total insurance offered, another such measure could be a set of dummy variables measuring the number of different deductibles and coinsurance rates offered by each insurer. A further measure of this variable could be the number of different policies offered by the insurer. The more diverse the product mix, the higher we would expect AC to be. AGE and SEX would be variables to indicate the influence of the insurer's clientele upon its costs.[g] TAXES would measure the differential effect on how each insurer is taxed and how taxation affects his average costs. SALES would be a variable which measured the extent of the selling effort of the insurer. One measure of this variable is the percent of total costs that selling costs represent. We would expect selling costs to be directly related to AC. WORK would be an estimate of the total work effort involved in the insurance transaction that was done by those other than the insuring organization. We would expect an inverse relation between this variable and AC. QUALITY would be a variable which measures the intensiveness of the claims review process. We would expect that an insurer who was careful about the validity of the claims presented to him would have a higher AC than one who was not careful. One measure of QUALITY might be the amount of time spent on each claim multiplied by the salary of the claims examiner. If empirical data were available for all of these variables for all insurers, a regression equation could standardize

[g]It is well known that the initial planners of Medicare realized that insuring the aged presents problems of an informational and understanding nature.

for each of these influences upon administrative costs and enable us to estimate the *net* effect of each independent variable upon *AC* for all insurers. The fundamental conclusion emanating from this discussion is that the existing body of data does not provide the analytical base for comparing the performances of the three main types of insurers. A more definitive study could be accomplished provided that an adequate data base were developed.

The Concept of Output and Cost Used for Empirical Purposes

In the chapters which follow we will attempt to estimate separate average cost functions for the three major insuring entities. Average cost implies that costs be presented in reference to output. For example, if we were to estimate average cost functions for the steel industry, production costs would be measured per metric ton of steel or per some other tangible measure of output. One of the reasons that the service sector of the economy has been so sadly neglected by economists is that the output of the service sector is not tangible and is, consequently, difficult to conceptualize and measure.

The most visible output which the health insurance industry produces is risk abatement. The industry sells contingent claims against future losses of wealth to individuals due to morbidity and pays those claims. It also sells other services such as information. Therefore, the ideal measure of output for the industry would be the amount of claims payments plus the real value of the other services which it provides.[h] This information is not available. Data on the amounts of claims paid are publsihed but data on the value of other services provided are not. A possible proxy measure of health insurance output would be the total sales of the industry, which is premiums written, but this measure overstates output because it includes profits and additions to reserves; one could argue that profits are not output, although additions to reserves might be viewed as output because they safeguard the future viability of making claims payments. But one could also argue that profits are a part of output because in a competitive industry profits are normal profits and thus a return to capital; the measure of national output, Gross National Product, contains profits. If claims payments

[h]Even this measure is not ideal for any point in time and the reason why it is not ideal illustrates once again the difficulties in measuring output for service industries. Take two insurers who are identical in every respect, even in their clientele. Due to the randomness of morbidity, Insurer A must pay a large claim at one point while Insurer B pays no claim. Is Insurer A producing more output than Insurer B? By the above measure of output contained in the text, he is doing so. Yet, both insurers have accepted contingent claims from their clientele and because of this contractual arrangement are really supplying identical outputs. In this case, the relevant concept of output would be premiums paid minus that portion of premiums paid as profits to the insurers. In a wider time-frame, no conceptual difficulty arises because claims paid plus the real value of services rendered ought to exactly equal premiums paid less profits for all insurers.

alone are used as a measure of output, output is understated because the value of services provided other than risk abatement is not included. A third possible measure of output would be claims payments plus administrative costs. The rationale for using this measure is that the amount of administrative costs captures the value of all of the services provided by the insurer over and above risk abatement. The problem with this measure is that there is no way of knowing whether a high value for it means that a producer is supplying more services or better quality services, or is merely inefficient relative to a producer having a low value for this measure. If competition does not produce equal efficiency on the part of all insurers, this measure will bias output in favor of the inefficient. In spite of the limitations of this third concept of output, we have chosen it as the best possible one given the data that are available.

By definition, average cost equals production costs divided by output. In the case of health insurance, production costs are administrative costs; these costs represent the value of the real resources consumed in the production of the output. The output of the industry is claims payments plus other services whose value can be represented by administrative costs. Therefore, our average cost variable may be represented as:

(a) average cost = administrative costs/(Claims payments + administrative costs)

Alternative specifications of the average cost variable would be:

(b) average cost = administrative costs/claims payments
(c) average cost = administrative costs/premiums written.[i]

In the chapters which follow, we report only those equations which use (a) or variants of it. When (b) or (c) were used, our basic results did not change.

Notes

1. Most intermediate microeconomic theory texts have an adequate discussion of the ensuring discussion for the two dimensional case. For a generalization, see *The Neoclassical Theory of Production and Distribution* (London: Cambridge University Press, 1971), chapters 6 and 7.

2. David B. Houston and Richard M. Simon, "Economies of Scale in Financial Institutions: A Study of Life Insurance," *Econometrica*, 38, No. 6, November 1970, pp. 856-864.

3. In principle, the analysis above should be conducted for the multi-product

[i]For Blue Cross-Blue Shield, the denominator of (c) would be earned subscription income; for Medicare, the denominator of (c) would be total expenditures.

firm. Although the Kuhn-Tucker analysis must replace the classical nonlinear mathematical programming approach, the economic principles are not elusive. For an excellent treatment, see Ferguson, *Neoclassical Theory* (1971, Chapter 10). In practice, the difficulty lies in appropriately defining the output and estimating what may be non-separable cost functions.

4. The basis of this discussion can be found in Robert A. Schuchardt, *Managerial Accounting in the Property and Casualty Business* (Cincinnati: The National Underwriter Company, 1969).

5. David B. Houston and Richard M. Simon, *loc. cit.*, pp. 856-864.

6. See, The National Underwriter Company, 1971, *Argus Chart of Health Insurance* (Cincinnati: The National Underwriter Company, 1971).

7. Louis S. Reed, *Financial Experiences of Health Insurance Organizations in the United States*, Social Security Administration, Office of Research and Statistics, Research Report No. 12, 1965, p. 39.

8. *Medical Economics* reports that, in 1971, 69 percent of all physicians devoted some time to working on insurance forms. Of these physicians, 10 percent spent five hours or more per week, 16 percent spent three to four hours, and 74 percent spent one to two hours. See, Arthur Owens, "Time Well Spent?: New Norms Will Help You See," *Medical Economics*, December, 1971.

2 The Commercial Insurers

In 1971, the commercial insurance companies wrote \$12.8 billion in accident and health premiums and accounted for 56 percent of non-government health insurance sold. Of the \$9.1 billion in benefits paid, \$1.7 billion was for loss of income insurance.[1] Both individual and group coverage were offered. The *Argus Chart* lists twenty-three different forms of individual health coverage and twenty-five different forms of group health coverage.[2] The individual and group policies are listed in Table 2-1.

The *Argus Chart* provides the following percentage breakdown for *individual* health insurance sold: non-cancellable, 16.2 percent; guaranteed renewable, 40.5 percent; nonrenewable for stated reasons, 5.3 percent; and other, 38.1 percent. Unfortunately, no breakdown is given for group health insurance.

The cost of administering commercial health insurance varies widely depending upon whether the policies involve group or individual insurance. The volume of insurance written by the company also seems to have a significant impact on administrative costs. Table 2-2 presents the administrative expense experience of the largest commercial firms selling health insurance for the years 1968-1970. The ratios are averages for the three-year period and they are accompanied by their coefficients of variation.[a] The cell sizes in Table 2-2 were selected so that an approximately even amount of premium volume is contained in each cell as shown in column five of the table.[b] With group health insurance, there appears to be a negative correlation between the size of premium volume and the size of administrative costs, expressed as a percentage of premiums written. For individual health insurance, the inverse relationship between premium volume and administrative costs does not appear to be as clear-cut but the operating ratio does become smaller as premium volume increases. In no individual health insurance premium class are administrative expenses as a percentage of premiums written smaller than the group health insurance administrative expense ratios.

Some of these relationships are not surprising. Because selling costs are such a large component of individual health insurance costs and because other costs,

Some of the ideas in this chapter first appeared in Roger D. Blair, Jerry R. Jackson and Ronald J. Vogel, "Economies of Scale in the Administration of Health Insurance," *Review of Economics and Statistics*, May 1975, ©1975 by the President and Fellows of Harvard College.

[a]The coefficient of variation is the standard error divided by the mean, $\sigma/\overline{X}$. It standardizes the variation present by expressing the variation as a percentage of the mean.

[b]The computer program which selects the number and sizes of the cells through an iterative process was written by Stephen Harden.

Table 2-1
Health Insurance Contracts Written

Individual coverages	Group coverages
1. Accident Only	1. Association (Under Master Contract)
2. Automobile Accident	2. Business Overhead Expense (Assn.)
3. Aviation Accident	3. Campers
4. Business Overhead Expense	4. Credit Unions, Blanket
5. Optionally Renewable	5. Credit Installment, Blanket
6. Credit Installment	6. Dental
7. Dental	7. Diagnostic Service
8. Guaranteed Renewable (Adjustable Premium)	8. Employee
a. Hospital-Surgical	9. Franchise
b. Major Medical	10. Hospital and Surgical
c. Loss of Time	11. Loss of Time
9. Hospital and Surgical	a. Long-Term Disability
10. Loss of Time	12. Major Medical
11. Major Medical	13. Medical Expense (Regular)
12. Medical Expense (regular)	14. Nursing Home Care
13. Monthly Premium	15. Poliomyelitis-Specified Disease
14. Mortgage Protection	16. Reinsurance
15. Newspaper Accident	17. School Children, Blanket
16. Non-Cancellable	18. Small Group (Under 25 Persons)
a. Hospital-Surgical	19. Sports Teams
b. Major Medical	20. Statutory Disability, California
c. Loss of Time	21. Statutory Disability, N.J.
17. Poliomyelitis-Specified Disease	22. Statutory Disability, N.Y.
18. Railroad Installment	23. Students, Blanket
19. Reinsurance	24. Transportation, Blanket
20. Specified Rates	25. Volunteer Firemen, Blanket
21. Substandard (Premium Rated)	
22. Travel, Limited	
23. Weekly Premium, Industrial	

Source: The National Underwriter Company, *1971 Argus Chart of Health Insurance* (Cincinnati: The National Underwriter Company, 1971).

e.g., claims handling, would be comparable to group health insurance, the fixed-cost component of individual health insurance would be proportionately less than for group health insurance. Because types of operation where fixed costs are large generally enjoy economies of scale, one might suspect that there would be greater economies of scale in group health insurance than in individual

Table 2-2
Administrative Expense Ratios and Coefficients of Variation, Commercial Health Insurers, 1968-1970

Premium volume (in thousands)	Number of firms	Administrative Costs ÷ Premiums Mean ratio	Coefficient of variation	Total premium volume in size class (in thousands)
		Individual insurance		
0-$4,162	173	51.5%	.51	293,316
4,163-7,650	50	46.1	.24	339,200
7,651-13,800	29	47.8	.15	253,166
13,801-25,000	17	45.8	.16	320,714
25,001-41,000	9	42.4	.18	316,814
41,001-60,000	7	45.9	.13	298,993
60,001-120,000	4	40.9	.18	301,459
120,001-150,000	2	43.4	.05	296,737
150,001-200,000	2	37.8	.13	295,743
200,001-300,000	1	36.0	0	297,700
		Group Insurance		
0-$18,000	197	24.5	.65	894,953
18,801-57,000	31	16.5	.37	768,213
57,001-132,000	12	12.7	.17	1,168,914
132,001-300,000	6	11.2	.52	880,084
300,001-500,000	2	10.9	.06	1,081,825
500,001-700,000	2	9.4	.05	1,012,912
700,001-850,000	1	8.8	0	982,600
850,001-950,000	1	9.6	0	985,784

Source: The National Underwriter Company, *1971 Argus Chart of Health Insurance*, (Cincinnati: The National Underwriter Company, 1971).

health insurance. What is difficult to explain are some of the relatively large coefficients of variation which indicate that in some premium volume classes for group and individual health insurance there is a fairly wide dispersion of administrative cost ratios around the mean.[c] Some of the firms with larger premium volume seem to show less variation in their administrative costs than

[c]The dispersion might indicate that all firms are doing well and that there are some firms which are more efficient than others and possibly some imperfection in the market. An alternative explanation might be that some firms are infra-marginal, i.e., profits ≷ 0 for firms away from the mean.

some of the smaller premium-volume firms, but no clear-cut pattern emerges.

Tables 2-3 through 2-6 provide a breakdown of the components of administrative costs expressed as a percentage of premiums earned for twenty-six of the thirty largest health insurers. It would be preferable to have more detail, but the Annual Statement filed in the District of Columbia and the individual states only requires that the following four categories of administrative expense be given: (1) total operating expenses, (2) taxes, licenses and fees, (3) general insurance expenses, and (4) net commission. Categories (2), (3), and (4) are mutually exclusive and exhaustive subsets of (1). As can be seen in Table 2-3, operating expenses vary widely by company and by type of insurance offered. In the preponderance of cases, group insurance is less costly to administer than individual insurance. Interestingly, however, even among these large companies, which accounted for 70 percent and 41 percent of the group and individual commercial health insurance written in 1971, group operating results vary widely. Individual insurance is much more expensive to administer than group insurance. The data show that the average administrative expenses for non-cancellable and guaranteed renewable policies exceed 50 percent. Table 2-4 indicates that taxes are not a source of variation because taxes as a percentage of premiums earned remain fairly constant by type of insurance and by company. General insurance expenses contribute less to the variation than do commissions and when one contrasts Tables 2-5 and 2-6, it becomes apparent that the greatest divergence in practice seems to occur in the area of commissions. Table 2-5 is of interest because it offers some indication of what commercial insurance administrative expenses would be if there were no taxes and no commissions. The average administrative cost for commercial group health insurance is comparable to that of Blue Cross-Blue Shield.

Because the underlying internal practices of each individual company are probably consistent across product lines, one might reasonably expect systematic variation of administrative costs by line of business by company. In other words, if a company has high administrative costs for one or two types of insurance relative to the costs of those kinds of insurance for other companies, its administrative costs for its other lines of insurance would be higher relative to those of other companies. To test this hypothesis, analysis of variance was applied by comparing the administrative costs of the seven different forms of insurance, by company, against each other. The results of this test are contained in Table 2-7. The F statistic, which the analysis of variance produces, is obtained by dividing the variance among groups by the variance within groups. In applying this statistical test, our reasoning was as follows: if a company administers all forms of individual insurance as cheaply or as expensively as group insurance, then the variance within groups will be low. The variance among groups appears to be large when one reads Tables 2-3 through 2-6. A high F statistic would mean that the variance among groups was greater than the variance within groups, confirming that the twenty-six health insurance companies have systematic differences in administrative costs. The contents of Table 2-7 indicate that the null hypothesis cannot be rejected[d] for total operating expenses, general insurance expenses, and net commissions because the respective F ratios are low, .474, 1.057, and 1.302 and they are only significant at the .984, .402, and .175 levels.

Regression Analysis

In order to test for the existence of economies of scale and in order to determine what independent variables contribute to the variations in commercial administrative costs, a single equation least-squares regression technique was used. This technique is useful because it allows one to fit relationships between a dependent variable, such as operating costs, and a series of independent variables, such as size, product mix, and other factors that influence operating costs. The resultant coefficient of each independent variable reveals the *net* effect of that variable upon the dependent variable, holding all other independent variables constant.

A recent analysis of thirteen proposed national health insurance bills found that ten of the bills include the existing industry to one degree or another.[3] This strategy makes sense because of the expertise and machinery that presently reside within the health insurance industry. If such a strategy is adopted, however, the fundamental problem of allocating the administrative responsibility remains. As noted above, among the health insuring organizations there exists wide disparity in the average costs of administering their health insurance business. Ideally, designation of responsibility for administering any national health insurance program should be based upon efficiency considerations. To the extent that economies of scale are present within the administrative function of existing health insurers, centralization in a few firms can be justified. In contrast, if economies of scale are not present, administrative responsibility should be decentralized on efficiency grounds.

In order to examine whether centralized administration of national health insurance is feasible, we have attempted to fit average cost functions that will accommodate constant or decreasing costs.[4] As the measure of average administrative costs previously discussed in Chapter 1, we have used total operating costs divided by claims payments plus administrative costs (OPCOST). Claims payment plus administrative costs (P) has been selected as the measure of output size, which is analogous to using dollar sales volume less profits as a proxy for output. This procedure is strictly legitimate if output is homogeneous and competitive pressures compel the various firms to charge the same price.[5] We

---

[d]The null hypothesis states that there is *no* systematic relation between the variations perceived in Tables 2-3 through 2-6.

Table 2-3
Total Operating Expenses as a Percentage of Premiums After Dividends, by Type of Insurance and Company, 1971

Company	All forms of health insurance	Group accident and health	Collectively Renewable	Non-cancellable	Guaranteed renewable	Non-Renewable for stated reasons	Other accident	All Other
Aetna Life and Casualty	10.8	9.6	64.9	85.1	53.0	9.6	39.9	33.6
Travelers	11.1	8.9	29.4	53.8	51.0	18.4	38.0	56.2
Metropolitan Life	16.0	9.8	47.7	58.4	48.0	33.7	42.7	31.7
Prudential	16.5	10.3	20.9	51.4	47.9	24.5	47.6	16.6
Equitable Society	12.6	10.7	None	72.9	77.3	33.2	None	None
Connecticut General Life	11.9	10.8	45.9	58.8	54.1	18.1	37.6	19.8
Mutual of Omaha	26.4	9.0	32.0	24.2	38.6	34.8	51.0	39.3
John Hancock Mutual Life	14.7	10.8	None	67.6	60.3	None	None	22.4
Provident Life and Accident, Tenn.	12.3	7.9	37.6	57.2	55.7	35.5	61.6	34.1
Bankers Life and Casualty	36.2	8.1	37.6	102.1	40.5	54.5	35.1	21.4
Occidental Life, California	11.0	8.0	43.0	70.0	56.0	49.0	30.0	37.0
New York Life	22.0	15.5	26.7	50.4	44.7	26.6	33.4	31.4
Lincoln National Life	13.3	9.9	62.3	49.7	49.3	None	49.2	24.4
Combined Insurance Company	44.3	33.6	45.1	None	45.1	45.1	45.1	45.1
Union Labor Life	7.0	6.8	None	None	64.4	None	None	None
Bankers Life Company	36.2	8.1	37.6	102.1	40.5	59.5	35.1	21.4
Washington National	27.2	11.6	50.0	40.5	55.6	56.4	52.5	60.4
Union Mutual Life, Maine	17.1	13.8	30.9	62.7	51.7	None	None	None
Republic National Life	11.0	9.0	41.0	65.0	53.0	48.0	51.0	53.0
Pacific Mutual Life	14.0	10.0	None	None	52.0	None	46.0	39.0

General American Life	11.8	9.7	8.7	45.8	46.7	54.2	53.7	15.5
United Insurance, Illinois	49.2	19.7	None	51.2	92.0	48.4	50.6	53.6
Allstate	14.5	8.1	None	None	109.2	None	33.0	70.5
Continental Insurance	24.1	20.5	26.8	53.3	46.6	40.8	28.9	30.2
Mutual of New York	28.6	19.7	39.2	54.3	54.3	16.3	None	None
Great West Life	15.6	13.6	None	78.6	72.0	None	38.3	46.5
Average	19.8	12.1	38.3	61.6	56.1	37.2	42.9	36.5

Source: *Annual Statement* of each company filed at the District of Columbia Department of Insurance.

Table 2-4
Taxes, Licenses, and Fees as a Percentage of Premiums After Dividends, by Type of Insurance and Company, 1971

Company	All forms of health insurance	Group accident and health	Collectively renewable	Non-cancellable	Guaranteed renewable	Non-renewable for stated reasons	Other accident	All Other
Aetna Life and Casualty	2.6	2.6	3.5	4.3	3.4	1.9	2.8	3.2
Travelers	2.5	2.5	2.7	3.6	3.3	2.9	2.6	4.8
Metropolitan Life	2.8	2.6	3.5	4.5	3.8	3.4	3.6	2.8
Prudential	2.5	2.3	2.5	3.7	3.5	3.7	None	3.3
Equitable Society	2.7	2.6	None	4.9	5.8	4.3	None	None
Connecticut General Life	2.4	2.4	1.8	3.8	3.5	2.3	2.2	2.7
Mutual of Omaha	2.4	2.2	2.6	3.4	2.5	2.5	3.1	2.2
John Hancock Mutual Life	2.4	2.3	None	4.7	4.2	None	None	2.0
Provident Life and Accident, Tenn.	2.3	2.2	2.6	2.9	3.1	2.8	2.5	2.5
Bankers Life and Casualty	2.8	1.6	2.8	2.8	3.0	None	2.8	2.9
Occidental Life, California	2.0	2.0	3.0	4.0	3.0	2.0	3.0	3.0
New York Life	2.8	2.6	3.3	3.9	3.7	3.6	3.4	3.3
Lincoln National Life	2.3	2.2	3.2	0.8	3.2	None	2.0	2.7
Combined Insurance Company	2.6	2.6	2.6	None	2.6	2.6	2.6	2.6
Union Labor Life	2.4	2.4	None	None	3.3	None	None	None
Bankers Life Company	2.8	1.6	2.8	2.8	3.0	None	2.8	2.9
Washington National	2.4	1.9	2.9	3.1	3.1	3.1	3.1	4.3
Union Mutual Life, Maine	2.3	2.2	2.4	2.7	3.1	None	None	None
Republic National Life	2.0	2.0	2.0	3.0	3.0	2.0	1.0	2.0
Pacific Mutual Life	3.0	3.0	None	None	3.0	None	3.0	3.0

General American Life	2.1	2.2	2.6	2.3	2.1	2.5	2.4	1.0
United Insurance, Illinois	3.1	0.4	None	3.7	4.5	2.6	2.7	3.6
Allstate	3.1	2.7	None	None	9.4	None	2.8	4.7
Continental Insurance	2.5	2.4	2.6	2.8	2.8	2.6	2.6	2.6
Mutual of New York	2.8	2.4	2.2	4.4	3.9	4.6	None	None
Great West Life	2.3	2.2	None	3.9	4.3	None	3.9	4.2
Average	2.5	2.2	2.7	3.5	3.6	2.9	2.7	3.0

Source: *Annual Statement* of each company filed at the District of Columbia Department of Insurance.

Table 2-5
General Insurance Expenses as a Percentage of Premiums After Dividends, by Type of Insurance and Company, 1971

Company	All forms of health insurance	Group accident and health	Collectively renewable	Non-cancellable	Guaranteed renewable	Non-renewable for stated reasons	Other accident	All other
Aetna Life and Casualty	6.6	5.9	45.8	51.2	34.5	7.8	16.5	17.3
Travelers	6.6	5.2	14.6	24.7	29.4	13.4	19.6	37.7
Metropolitan Life	10.8	7.0	28.4	34.8	31.3	23.6	34.5	21.4
Prudential	9.9	6.4	10.5	31.6	27.5	21.3	8.6	13.3
Equitable Society	8.4	6.9	None	52.5	53.0	28.7	None	None
Commercial General Life	7.0	6.4	None	33.5	33.6	9.6	12.7	14.7
Mutual of Omaha	11.3	4.7	15.9	12.6	15.0	16.9	14.4	16.0
John Hancock Mutual Life	10.0	7.5	None	42.8	38.2	None	None	21.4
Provident Life and Accident, Tenn.	6.5	4.5	20.3	24.3	26.3	18.7	21.4	20.6
Bankers Life and Casualty	17.5	6.4	13.9	63.9	18.7	None	28.9	13.3
Occidental Life, California	6.0	4.0	30.0	39.0	33.0	34.0	14.0	19.0
New York Life	13.7	9.3	13.7	33.3	29.5	23.1	23.2	21.4
Lincoln National Life	6.0	4.5	38.6	18.8	24.4	None	14.6	11.8
Combined Insurance Company	19.2	24.4	18.6	None	18.6	18.6	18.6	18.6
Union Labor Life	3.8	3.6	None	None	58.6	None	None	None
Bankers Life Company	17.5	6.4	13.9	63.9	18.7	0	28.9	13.3
Washington National	15.9	7.6	32.1	30.7	30.8	30.6	32.3	29.3
Union Mutual Life, Maine	8.2	6.4	12.5	32.6	29.1	None	None	None
Republic National Life	6.0	5.0	20.0	28.0	26.0	24.0	11.0	23.0
Pacific Mutual Life	9.0	6.0	None	None	35.0	None	30.0	29.0

General American Life	7.2	6.3	6.1	19.2	23.1	24.3	24.9	6.2
United Insurance, Illinois	15.9	4.3	None	17.5	25.9	14.8	15.4	17.8
Allstate	8.0	5.0	None	None	55.3	None	16.9	27.7
Continental Insurance	12.2	11.4	11.7	26.9	24.4	15.3	11.2	11.9
Mutual of New York	17.4	12.2	23.8	31.3	33.3	11.8	None	None
Great West Life	8.7	7.0	None	53.6	49.8	None	33.0	42.6
Average	10.4	7.1	20.6	34.9	31.7	19.8	20.5	20.3

Source: *Annual Statement* of each company filed at the District of Columbia Department of Insurance.

Table 2-6
Net Commissions as a Percentage of Premiums After Dividends, by Type of Insurance and Company, 1971

Company	All forms of health insurance	Group accident and health	Collectively renewable	Non-cancellable	Guaranteed renewable	Non-renewable for stated reasons	Other accident	All other
Aetna Life and Casualty	1.6	1.2	15.5	29.6	15.1	None	20.6	13.1
Travelers	2.0	1.1	12.2	25.5	18.3	2.1	15.8	13.6
Metropolitan Life	2.3	0.1	15.6	18.9	12.7	6.5	3.8	7.3
Prudential	4.1	1.6	7.9	16.1	16.9	.5	39.0	None
Equitable Society	1.6	1.1	None	15.5	18.5	.3	None	None
Commercial General Life	2.5	2.1	44.2	21.5	17.0	6.3	22.8	2.5
Mutual of Omaha	12.6	2.1	13.5	8.2	21.0	15.5	33.6	21.1
John Hancock Mutual Life	2.3	1.0	None	20.1	17.9	None	None	None
Provident Life and Accident, Tenn.	3.5	1.2	14.7	30.0	26.3	14.0	37.7	10.9
Bankers Life and Casualty	15.9	.2	20.9	35.4	18.8	54.5	3.4	5.1
Occidental Life, California	3.0	2.0	10.0	27.0	19.0	13.0	13.0	15.0
New York Life	5.4	3.6	9.8	13.3	11.6	None	6.9	6.7
Lincoln National Life	5.0	3.2	20.5	28.1	21.7	None	32.5	9.8
Combined Insurance Company	22.5	6.6	23.9	None	23.9	23.9	23.9	24.0
Union Labor Life	.8	.8	None	None	2.5	None	None	None
Bankers Life Company	15.9	.2	20.9	35.4	18.8	54.5	3.4	5.1
Washington National	8.9	2.1	15.1	6.7	21.7	22.7	17.1	26.8
Union Mutual Life, Maine	6.6	5.2	16.0	27.4	19.5	None	None	None
Republic National Life	3.0	2.0	18.0	34.0	24.0	22.0	39.0	27.0
Pacific Mutual Life	2.0	1.0	None	None	14.0	None	13.0	7.0

General American Life	2.5	1.2	0.0	24.3	21.5	27.4	26.4	8.3
United Insurance, Illinois	30.2	15.0	None	30.1	61.6	31.1	32.4	32.3
Allstate	3.4	.4	None	None	44.5	None	13.3	38.1
Continental Insurance	9.4	6.7	12.5	23.6	19.4	22.9	15.1	15.7
Mutual of New York	8.3	5.1	13.3	18.6	17.1	None	None	None
Great West Life	4.6	4.4	None	21.1	17.9	None	1.4	−0.3
Average	6.9	2.7	16.9	23.2	20.8	19.8	19.7	14.5

Source: *Annual Statement* of each company filed at the District of Columbia Department of Insurance.

Table 2-7
Analysis of Variance, Operating Expense Ratios for 26 of the Largest Health Insurers, 1971

Type of operating expense as a percentage of premiums earned	Sum of squares	Mean square	Degress of freedom	F-Ratio	Significance level
(1) Total operating expenses					
Between groups	556,776	22,271	25	.474	.984
Within groups	6,065,437	47,019	129		
(2) General insurance expenses					
Between groups	446,408	17,856	25	1.057	.402
Within groups	2,128,085	16,890	126		
(3) Net commissions					
Between groups	455,756	18,230	25	1.302	.175
Within groups	1,721,569	13,996	123		

Source: Data contained in Tables 2-3, 2-5, and 2-6.

have specified the following alternative cost functions: (1) linear, OPCOST = $a + bP$; (2) reciprocal, OPCOST = $a + b\ (1/P)$; (3) reciprocal logarithmic, OPCOST = $a + b(1/1nP)$; and (4) logarithmic, OPCOST = $a + b1nP$. With the exception of the linear form, these functions are monotonically decreasing at increasing rates provided the regression coefficient is positive for the reciprocal and reciprocal logarithmic forms and negative for the logarithmic form.[e]

Although we expect the size of the firm to be an important explanatory variable for OPCOST, we recognize that other factors also may be important determinants. In the health insurance industry, a relatively few large firms handle the majority of the business. In fact, in our sample of 327 firms the largest 26 firms accounted for some 70 percent of the group health business and 40 percent of the individual health business. To examine whether the structure of the industry affects the average cost curve, we have introduced a dummy variable L into the regression equation, which assumes a value of one if the firm sells in excess of \$100 million in premiums. The effect of including L is to allow the intercept to vary between large and small firms. If the coefficient is statistically significant, it should be added to the intercept term for large firms. In addition, the slope of the average administrative cost function may also be different for large as opposed to small firms. To admit this possibility, we have included an interaction dummy variable $L{\cdot}f(P)$, where $f(P)$ denotes one of the four functional forms specified at the beginning of this section. If this coefficient is significant, it should be added to the coefficient of $f(P)$. The main purpose of including these shift variables is to account for X-efficiency considerations. Because there was not a clear clustering of firms well below the cut-off point of \$100 million in premiums, we have also attempted to fit an average cost function in which L and $L{\cdot}f(P)$ are deleted.

In addition to size-related variables, several other explanatory variables have been included. Perhaps the most important additional consideration in health insurance is the effect of group policies. One should expect that the greater the percentage of total health business accounted for by group business, the lower will be the firm's administrative costs. There are two main factors at work here: (1) The greater the percentage of group business, the less diverse are the administrative functions, which should result in greater efficiencies; (2) Perhaps more importantly, many group policies provide for much of the administrative functions' being performed by the customer. This would obviously lower the costs to the insurer. For these reasons, we have included the variable GI/T, group health insurance premiums divided by total health insurance premiums. Since, the motivation of this study lies in the imminence of national health insurance, it is important to control for group insurance. The result may not be unambiguous, however, because the higher is GI/T, the more specialized is the firm in group health insurance. But group health insurance is less costly to administer. Thus, there will be a specialization effect plus a group effect.

[e]That is $d\ [\text{OPCOST}]/dP < 0$ and $d^2\ \text{OPCOST}/dP^2 > 0$.

Suppose GI/T approaches zero. In a linear regression $\frac{d(AC)}{d(GI/T)} < 0$ implies that an increase in group business will reduce AC. But if GI/T is close to zero, this indicates specialization in *individual* insurance. Thus, the sign of the coefficient of GI/T might change from + to – as the ratio changes from low values to high values.

One should also expect that specialization leads to greater efficiencies, and, thus, to lower costs. To the extent that firms specialize in health insurance, their regular employees would have a greater opportunity to specialize and its selling strategy could become more concentrated. Thus, it would be desirable to include a measure of the extent of specialization in health insurance. Although ideal measures are unavailable, we have attempted to use health reserves as a percentage of total reserves, HR/TR.[f] On a priori grounds, we would expect the coefficient to have a negative sign. A further refinement is possible to control for firm type. The data source classifies the commercial health insurers into four categories: (1) Health Insurance Specialty Company, (2) Life and Health Company, (3) Casualty Company, and (4) Multiple Line Company. A set of dummy variables FT_i, $i = 2,3,4$, was included in the regression equation to determine what differential effect company type might have on OPCOST.[g] Due to the rather arbitrary classification scheme, it is difficult to assign a priori signs to these coefficients, but one might expect the Health Insurance Specialty Company to have lower average administrative costs.

Finally, we have also included a corporate form dummy variable S, which assumes the value one for stock firms and zero for mutual firms. Since the firms claim that corporate form makes a difference, it should be of some interest to determine whether it does. For our purposes, however, there should be little, if any, difference because both types of firms have an incentive to minimize costs.[h] Presumably, a significant coefficient on this variable will reflect differences in managerial ability.

Thus, the general functional form of our model appears as

$$\begin{aligned} \text{OPCOST} = {} & b_0 + b_1 f(P) + b_2 L + b_3 L \cdot f(P) + b_4 \text{HR/TR} \\ & + b_5 S + b_6 FT_2 + b_7 FT_3 + b_8 FT_4 + b_9 GI/T + u \end{aligned}$$

where $f(P)$ takes on one of the functional forms specified above and u is a stochastic disturbance term, which is assumed to be homoskedastic. We have also

[f] It would probably be more desirable to use health premiums written as a percentage of total premiums written. Unfortunately, the available data do not allow us to do this as we do not have total premiums written for each firm.

[g] By omitting the first firm type, Health Insurance Specialty Company, the coefficients on the FT_i measure the differential firm effects with respect to the first firm type.

[h] If the firms in our sample are not all cost minimizers, then one is not justified in assuming that the regression will trace out the cost envelope.

estimated an average administrative cost function from which L, $L \cdot f(P$, and HR/TR were deleted. The variables L and $L \cdot f(P)$ were deleted because of the absence of a clear clustering. The variable HR/TR was deleted because it is a somewhat ambiguous measure of specialization and because it is a bit redundant given the firm-type dummy variables.

The Data

The data for the regression analysis were taken from the 1971 *Argus Chart of Health Insurance,* (the ACHI).[6] The ACHI gives detailed data for 327 insurance companies which sell health insurance, for the years 1968-70, and the data in this source are broken down by total health insurance and individual health insurance, so that group results may also be derived. Of the original 327 observations, some had to be discarded because of inconsistencies in data reporting. Thus, we were left with a total sample of 307 observations for each year.

Table 2-8 contains frequency distributions of administrative expenses as a percentage of premiums written for the companies in our sample. The median expense ratio for individual insurance is 47.0 percent, while the comparable figure for group insurance is 18.8 percent. One can only speculate on the competitive implications of these relatively high expense ratios. As will be shown later, the Blue Cross-Blue Shield plans have much lower operating ratios. Furthermore, one could legitimately question why commercial firms with operating ratios well below the median do not lure business from firms well above the median. One reason why those companies with high operating expense ratios continue in business may lie in the previously used equation,

$$B = P - (A + C),$$

where B may be seen as a break-even point or a targeted level of profit, P is premiums, A is administrative costs, and C is claims costs. If an individual has a choice of being insured by company X or company Y, he may prefer company Y even though company Y's A/P ratio exceeds that of company X. This may occur because he is placed in a pool of insurees such that his net cost of insurance is lower with company Y than with company X, i.e., his P is lower because he is in a group under company Y's policy which has much better experience. This may help to explain why Blue Cross-Blue Shield has lost business to the commercials over time. Blue Cross-Blue Shield has tried, until the recent past, to community rate and those individuals with better experience have left the community pool and gone to the experience rated pools of the commercials. Thus, company Y and Blue Cross might have the exact absolute amount of A for two given groups of insurees of the same size, but because experience under Blue Cross's insurees

Table 2-8
Frequency Distribution of Administrative Expenses as a Percentage of Premiums Written, Commercial Insurers, 1968-1970

Administrative expenses as a percentage of premiums written	Number of insurance companies	
	Individual	Group
0-4.9	0	4
5-9.9	0	28
10-14.9	2	51
15-19.9	2	59
20-24.9	6	41
25-29.9	5	21
30-34.9	23	17
35-39.9	29	11
40-44.9	59	9
45-49.9	57	1
50-54.9	48	5
55-59.9	24	5
60-64.9	22	1
65-69.9	9	1
70-74.9	4	1
75-79.9	3	0
80-84.9	0	0
85-89.9	0	0
90-94.9	0	0
95-99.9	1	0
100 and over	4	1
Totals	298	256

Source: The National Underwriter Company, *1971 Argus Chart of Health Insurance,* (Cincinnati, The National Underwriter Company, 1971).

Note:

Individual Insurance	Group Insurance
Mode = 40-44.9%	Mode = 15-19.9%
Median* = 47%	Median* = 18.8%
Mean = 48.9%	Mean = 22.3%

*Estimated by the formula:

$$\text{Md} = \text{lower limit of Md class} + \text{Md class interval} \times \frac{\text{required number}}{\text{frequency of Md class}}$$

is so bad, C is larger, which necessitates a high P and, as a consequence, A/P is smaller than for company Y. But insurees are concerned with the costs of insurance, not with A/P ratios per se. Thus, the better risks will tend to leave Blue Cross-Blue Shield. This highlights the risks inherent in relying on A/P ratios to the exclusion of other factors.

Another reason may be a geographical one: the low-cost insurers may have failed to penetrate certain geographical areas and the high cost insurers are able to maintain regional monopolies. A final explanation may be that many consumers of health insurance are not knowledgeable consumers and are not aware that price differentials, due to differences in administrative costs, exist for the same kinds of coverage.[7] The National Underwriter's *Time-Saver* lists a plethora of policies at a plethora of prices and it could well be that the average consumer of health insurance may become confused in his choice of a health insurance policy. This last explanation, however, may not be appropriate for group health insurance. Purchasers of large group policies are more sophisticated than most purchasers of individual health insurance. One should expect them to know what kind of policy they want and at what price. For example, when the UAW is negotiating for group health insurance for their membership, insurance expertise is brought to bear. Leonard Woodcock, president of the UAW, has testified that health care benefit programs worth in excess of $725 million annually have been negotiated.[8] Since such benefits are received in lieu of wage increases, it is well worth the UAW's effort to develop and use expertise in this area of negotiations. Price competition in the group business may be one of the reasons why the median operating ratio for group health insurance is so much lower than that for individual insurance.

Regression Results[i]

The regression results for both variants of the four functional forms are presented in Tables 2-9, 2-10, 2-11 and 1-12. For all forms, the R^2 values fall between 0.53 and 0.61. Generally, the coefficient on $f(P)$ is highly statistically significant irrespective of functional form. Moreover, its sign indicates the presence of scale economies. The shift dummy variable, $L \cdot f(P)$, proved to be significant in only the linear form. The generally poor performance of this variable can be explained partially by the lack of a clear clustering of firms above and below the rather arbitrary delineation between large and small firms. The other shift dummy, L, was generally insignificant.

As one would expect, the group insurance specialization variable, GI/T, has a negative and statistically significant coefficient in each equation. This was anticipated on a priori grounds because group insurance is less costly to administer. In addition, many group policies provide for the customer's perform-

[i]Since we have time-series and cross-section observations, we attempted to pool our data. This effort proved disappointing. Part of the difficulty lies in our crucial assumption that claims payments plus administrative costs can be used as an output measure. In order to pool time-series and cross-section data, one must deflate the data. Two problems arise: (1) no single price index is wholly suitable and (2) insurance rates are set prior to knowing what medical charges will be. With respect to the latter, one cannot be sure that even a perfect price index would represent the adjustment factor used by the insurers in setting their rates.

Table 2-9
Regression Results: Linear Form*

		Constant	$f(P)$	$L \cdot f(P)$	L	GI/T	S	HR/TR	FT_2	FT_3	FT_4	R^2
OPCOST: Linear I $f(P) = p$	1968	.477	–.000001	.000001	–.068	–.003	.024	–.0001	.024	–.047	–.023	.597
		(30.49)[a]	(3.073)[a]	(2.864)[a]	(1.725)[c]	(18.796)[a]	(1.890)[c]	(.400)	(1.328)	(1.956)[b]	(.599)	
	1969	.480	–.000001	.000001	–.065	–.003	.026	–.0004	.026	–.021	–.118	.573
		(30.309)[a]	(2.827)[a]	(2.634)[a]	(1.791)[c]	(17.642)[a]	(2.067)[b]	(1.379)	(1.387)	(.839)	(2.956)[a]	
	1970	.505	–.000001	.000001	–.076	–.003	.021	–.0001	.024	–.032	–.061	.551
		(27.726)[a]	(3.551)[a]	(3.313)[a]	(1.942)[b]	(16.656)[a]	(1.441)	(.366)	(1.144)	(1.140)	(1.335)	
OPCOST: Linear II $f(P) = p$	1968	.464	–.0000002			–.003	.027		.025	–.045	–.023	.589
		(34.32)[a]	(3.152)[a]			(19.693)[a]	(2.113)[b]		(1.351)	(1.883)[c]	(.591)	
	1969	.459	–.0000002			–.003	.028		.029	–.025	–.116	557
		(33.143)[a]	(3.371)[a]			(18.367)[a]	(2.216)[b]		(1.538)	(1.000)	(2.873)[a]	
	1970	.486	–.0000002			–.003	.025		.024	–.027	–.058	.537
		(30.416)[a]	(3.263)[a]			(17.466)[a]	(1.666)[c]		(1.143)	(1.046)	(1.248)	

*Results are based upon 307 observations in each year. The *t*-values are given in parentheses below each estimate. Statistical significance at levels .01, .05, and .10 is indicated by a, b, and c, respectively.

Table 2-10
Regression Results: Reciprocal Form*

		Constant	$f(P)$	$L \circ f(P)$	L	GI/T	S	HR/TR	FT_2	FT_3	FT_4	R^2
OPCOST:	1968	.448 (28.690)[a]	44.034 (4.324)[a]	462.48 (.060)	−.055 (1.323)	−.003 (19.943)[a]	.029 (2.349)[b]	−.000004 (.016)	.210 (1.159)	−.053 (2.197)[b]	−.027 (.704)	.609
Reciprocal I	1969	.454 (24.758)[a]	40.550 (1.623)	173.430 (.023)	−.060 (1.461)	−.003 (17.200)[a]	.033 (2.594)[b]	−.0004 (1.360)	.019 (1.015)	−.024 (.950)	−.124 (3.063)[a]	.566
$f(P) = 1/P$	1970	.462 (21.771)[a]	75.055 (2.543)[b]	583.38 (.599)	−.088 (1.786)[c]	−.003 (16.091)[a]	.030 (2.058)[b]	−.00006 (.217)	.019 (.918)	−.040 (1.384)	−.065 (1.414)	.542
OPCOST:	1968	.446 (32.955)[a]	46.847 (4.652)[a]			−.003 (20.364)[a]	.030 (2.422)[b]		.013 (.743)	−.054 (2.303)[b]	−.025 (.643)	.604
Reciprocal II	1969	.436 (27.320)[a]	60.740 (2.496)[b]			−.003 (17.261)[a]	.035 (2.683)[a]		.013 (.697)	−.036 (1.440)	−.120 (2.946)[a]	.555
$f(P) = 1/P$	1970	.454 (24.981)[a]	90.210 (3.177)[a]			−.003 (16.408)[a]	.033 (2.265)[b]		.010 (473)	−.046 (1.601)	−.063 (1.359)	.536

*Results are based upon 307 observations in each year. The *t*-values are given in parentheses below each estimate. Statistical significance at levels .01, .05, and .10 is indicated by a, b, and c, respectively.

Table 2-11
Regression Results: Reciprocal Logarithmic Form*

		Constant	$f(P)$	$L \circ f(P)$	L	GI/T	S	HR/TR	FT_2	FT_3	FT_4	R^2
OPCOST: Reciprocal Logarithmic I $f(P) = 1/1nP$	1968	.254 (4.980)[a]	.753 (4.370)[a]	−.360 (.164)	.053 (.131)	−.003 (18.162)[a]	.026 (2.141)[b]	.00008 (.293)	.023 (1.250)	−.055 (2.302)[b]	−.029 (.755)	610
	1969	.318 (5.428)[a]	.540 (2.684)[a]	−.065 (.032)	−.017 (.046)	−.003 (16.625)[a]	.031 (2.433)[b]	−.00003 (1.106)	.022 (1.153)	−.025 (.993)	−.124 (3.102)[a]	.572
	1970	.247 (3.696)[a]	.871 (3.780)[a]	.701 (.294)	−.146 (.332)	−.003 (15.526)[a]	.027 (1.875)[c]	.00002 (.087)	.020 (.980)	−.039 (1.374)	−.066 (1.434)	.554
OPCOST: Reciprocal Logarithmic II $f(P) = 1/1nP$	1968	.247 (5.965)[a]	.784 (5.404)[a]			−.003 (18.472)[a]	.026 (2.156)[b]		.021 (1.227)	−.054 (2.330)[b]	−.029 (.764)	.613
	1969	.261 (5.572)[a]	.718 (4.343)[a]			−.003 (16.576)[a]	.030 (2.401)[b]		.021 (1.177)	−.033 (1.359)	−.123 (3.071)[a]	.572
	1970	.228 (4.327)[a]	.942 (5.018)[a]			−.003 (15.735)[a]	.028 (1.954)[c]		.018 (5.018)[a]	−.040 (1.444)	−.066 (1.448)	.557

*Results are based upon 307 observations in each year. The t-values are given in parentheses below each estimate. Statistical significance at levels .01, .05, and .10 is indicated by a, b, and c, respectively.

Table 2-12
Regression Results: Logarithmic Form*

		Constant	$f(P)$	$L \circ f(P)$	L	GI/T	S	HR/TR	FT_2	FT_3	FT_4	R^2
	1968	.648	–.050	.034	–.176	–.003	.025	.00004	.023	–.053	–.028	.606
OPCOST:		(13.632)[a]	(4.030)[a]	(.449)	(.433)	(18.000)[a]	(2.044)[b]	(.159)	(1.272)	(2.203)[b]	(.714)	
Logarithmic I	1969	.612	–.039	.019	–.115	–.003	.030	–.0003	.023	–.024	–.123	.574
$f(P) = 1nP$		(11.891)[a]	(2.893)[a]	(.275)	(.305)	(16.697)[a]	(2.334)[b]	(1.098)	(1.213)	(.966)	(3.077)[a]	
	1970	.711	–.061	.007	–.030	–.003	.025	.00002	.021	–.037	–.064	.555
		(12.157)[a]	(3.944)[a]	(.092)	(.070)	(15.626)[a]	(1.757)[c]	(.068)	(1.023)	(1.319)	(1.407)	
	1968	.639	–.048			–.003	.025		.025	–.051	–.028	.610
OPCOST:		(17.157)[a]	(5.134)[a]			(18.390)[a]	(2.038)[b]		(1.410)	(2.196)[b]	(.721)	
Logarithmic II	1969	.626	–.045			–.003	.028		.025	–.030	–.121	.576
$f(P) = 1nP$		(15.953)[a]	(4.637)[a]			(16.800)[a]	(2.252)[b]		(1.414)	(1.260)	(3.046)[a]	
	1970	.699	–.057			–.003	.025		.022	–.036	–.064	.560
		(15.622)[a]	(5.185)[a]			(15.945)[a]	(1.764)[c]		(1.087)	(1.324)	(1.419)	

*Results are based upon 307 observations in each year. The *t*-values are given in parentheses below each estimate. Statistical significance at levels .01, .05, and .10 is indicated by a, b, and c, respectively.

ing some of the administrative functions. There are two separate problems which suggest that the effects of group insurance specialization should be examined more carefully. First, the scale effect, exhibited by the coefficients on $f(P)$, may be confounded with the group variable. In other words, the large firms have a disproportionate share of the group business and the effect of this is appearing in the scale variable. We have examined this possibility and it appears to be unimportant. The simple correlation coefficient between premium volume and GI/T, while positive, is extremely small. Furthermore, we tested the scale effect using only individual business and again using only group business. The results confirm the existence of scale economies. Second, a more serious, and less easily resolved, problem concerns the size of the particular group. Intuition suggests that the average size of group covered is positively correlated with premium volume. In Table 2-13 we have presented some additional data that indicate the potential significance of this influence. These data show the administrative costs of various group sizes as a percentage of premiums earned. It is quite clear that as the size of the group increases, the administrative cost ratio falls rapidly. Thus, it would be extremely desirable to adjust for differences in the size of groups. Unfortunately, data that would permit such an adjustment are not available.

Generally, the health specialization variable, HR/TR, did not perform well. In nearly all cases, the coefficient was of the expected sign, but in no instance was it significant. This leads one to think that health insurance specialization fails to result in greater efficiency. In fact, this may be the case, i.e., that the administration of health insurance is not sufficiently different from other forms of insurance to lead to gains from specialization. Alternatively, the HR/TR variable may not be a good proxy for health insurance specialization. Reserve requirements vary for different types of insurance policies; therefore, the denominator of the ratio will vary for each firm depending upon the policy mix peculiar to the firm.

The firm type variables, FT_2, FT_3, and FT_4, were generally insignificant. Their performance did not change materially by the deletion of the HR/TR variable. The signs of the coefficients, however, suggest that the Life and Health Companies (FT_2) were less efficient than the Health Insurance Specialty Companies (FT_1), which, in turn, had higher average costs than either the Casualty (FT_3) or Multiple Line (FT_4) Companies. Inferences must be extremely tenuous due to the lack of statistical significance. Interestingly, the corporate form dummy, S, is positive and statistically significant in each instance. The positive sign of the coefficient indicates that administrative costs are higher for stock companies than for mutual firms. This result tends to deflate the claims of the stock companies that their profit-maximizing goals lead to higher levels of efficiency. Thus, the customers of mutual health insurance firms enjoy premium reductions through lower administrative costs as well as through returned profits.

Table 2-13
Cost of Group Medical Expense Insurance by Size of Case, United States, 1971

Size of case (number of lives)	Group administrative costs as a percentage of net premiums earned			
	Total	Premium taxes	Commissions	All other
250	8.7	2.1	1.5	5.1
500	7.9	2.1	1.1	4.7
1,000	7.0	2.1	0.7	4.2
2,500	6.2	2.1	0.4	3.7
10,000	5.3	2.1	0.2	3.0
50,000	5.0	2.1	0.1	2.8

Source: Health Insurance Association of America Survey of 14 insurance companies which wrote 52 percent of group health insurance in the United States in 1970.

Summary of Cross-Section Regressions

The primary purpose of this analysis was to investigate the possibility of economies of scale in the administration of commercial health insurance. Given the imminence of national health insurance and the apparent inclination to use the existing industry in administering it, the existence of scale economies has acquired public policy importance. In fitting one linear and three non-linear functional forms for average administrative costs, we found strong evidence of scale economies. From a conceptual standpoint, we should recall a problem that plagues all economies of scale studies: what appears to be scale efficiency may well be *X*-efficiency. In other words, the larger firms may have better management, which is reflected in lower costs. From the point of view of public policy, however, this distinction is not very important because our analysis indicates that the administrative function should tend to be centralized. Before leaping to a categorical conclusion, however, one must recognize that centralization would involve an enormous change in the operations of the firms involved.[j] Such a large, sudden change could alter the cost structure dramatically. Thus, a great deal of caution must be exercised in the interpretation of our results. Nonetheless, they suggest that significant decentralization of the administrative function would be undesirable.

The inference regarding the effect of corporate form is quite interesting. Although arguments can be made in either direction, we suspected that the profit-seeking stock firms would have had lower costs. The present analysis shows exactly the opposite: the mutual firms have lower average administrative costs.

Finally, the group insurance variable was in accord with a priori expectations. The larger the percentage of total health insurance accounted for by group insurance, the lower are average costs. In conjunction with the impression provided by the data in Table 2-13 it appears that further research should be done in this area.

Administrative Costs Over Time

Another method of analyzing administrative costs is to examine them over time. In a period of rapidly rising per capita health care costs, such as that experienced in the United States during the latter half of the 1960's and early 1970's, one would expect per capita insurance claims costs to increase at about the same rate because such claims reflect those rapidly escalating costs.[k] Administrative costs

[j]We estimated a quadratic cost function in an effort to determine where diseconomies of scale set it. The results indicate that only four firms operate at a scale where diseconomies may occur.

[k]This is true except to the extent that there are schedules for claims, e.g., indemnity plans have maximum pay for physician charges and room rates. But, over time these schedules increase, so even with indemnity plans, claims payments should follow increases in medical care costs with a lag.

per capita should not necessarily rise at the same time. The factors influencing inflation in the health care sector appear to be unique to that sector.[9] The commercial insurance industry, on the other hand, shares many of the characteristics of other service industries within the economy, so we would expect inflation in the insurance industry to move at the same rate as in the rest of the service sector. A priori reasoning also suggests that administrative costs per insuree would not go up at as rapid a rate as claims costs per insuree. As one member of the industry has pointed out, an envelope and a stamp are required for a claim payment whether that payment be for $1,000 or $100 and the available evidence seems to indicate that administrative expenses are more a function of the number of claims rather than the size of claims. (This statement will be documented empirically in subsequent sections of this study.) Thus, if the number of claims per insuree remains relatively constant, while the size of claims increases because of inflation in the health care sector, administrative costs per insuree ought to increase at a slower rate. Table 2-14 illustrates actual experience for the commercial health insurance industry as a whole for the period 1965-1970.[1] The table shows that administrative expenses per insuree increased 30.6 percent between 1965 and 1970, while claims costs and premiums earned increased 44.7 percent and 36.0 percent, respectively. The average annual rate of increase in administrative expenses was 5.1 percent while the average annual rate of increase of all items in the consumer price index for the same period was 3.9 percent. Claims costs per insuree went up at an average annual rate of 7.5 percent, while the medical care component of the consumer price index went up at an average annual rate of 5.8 percent and the hospital room rate component 14.6 percent.[10]

Because there are no published data available on the number of claims for commercial insurance during this period, it is not possible to ascertain whether this average annual increase in administrative costs, which is greater than the average annual increase in the "all items" component of the CPI, is due to increased claims or other factors. The "other factors" would include increased costs of claims handling and claims review, as well as increased selling costs.

The currently available statistical information on the commercial insurance industry makes it impossible to isolate all of those factors that influence the level of administrative costs. Operating-cost ratios for the commercial insurance companies are higher than those for Blue Cross-Blue Shield or for Medicare. As explained earlier, however, this does not necessarily imply that the commercial companies are less efficient. The services which they provide are different and their clientele, particularly the clientele with individual insurance, is different. The commercial companies offer a more valid benefit structure and consequently claims handling costs are higher. From a social point of view, the benefits of a wider range of consumer choice may make up for the higher costs of claims handling.[11] It might be argued that selling costs are excessive, but

[1]Unfortunately, data on a company-by-company basis could not be obtained. The Health Insurance Association of America does not release such data because of alleged competitive conditions within the industry.

Table 2-14
Premiums, Claims, and Expenses per Insuree, Commercial Insurance Companies, 1965-1970

(1) Year	(2) Number of persons with hospital expense protection, all insurance companies (in thousands)[1]	(3) Premiums earned (in thousands)[2]	(4) Claims incurred (in thousands)[2]	(5) Expenses incurred (in thousands)[2]	(6) (3) + (2) Premiums earned per insuree	(7) (4) + (2) Claims costs per insuree	(8) (5) ÷ (2) Administrative expenses per insuree
1965	93,723	$7,643,547	$5,810,325	$1,744,916	$81.55	$61.99	$18.62
1966	97,404	8,250,304	6,223,368	1,871,873	84.70	63.98	19.22
1967	100,298	8,879,811	6,679,642	1,996,373	88.53	66.60	19.90
1968	104,408	9,883,750	7,606,391	2,258,545	94.66	72.85	21.63
1969	108,508	10,906,188	8,548,945	2,462,259	100.51	78.79	22.69
1970	112,575	12,481,118	10,094,786	2,736,665	110.87	89.67	24.31
Percentage change:							
1967-1970	12.2	40.5	52.6	37.0	25.2	34.6	22.2
1965-1970	20.1	63.2	73.7	56.8	36.0	44.7	30.6

Sources:
1. National Underwriter Company, *1971 Argus Chart of Health Insurance* (Cincinnati: National Underwriter, 1966-71).
2. Health Insurance Institute, *Source Book of Health Insurance Data*, (New York: Health Insurance Institute, 1971).

again, a portion of those selling costs contained in commissions is payment for the services of an agent or broker, services which one might not obtain from Blue Cross-Blue Shield or from Medicare. Another portion related to advertising and informing the public.

Ultimately the question of whether the commercial carriers are inefficient reduces to the question of freedom of consumer choice. If the multiplicity of policies actually hinders consumer choice and confuses the consumer, then the outcome of the competitive process in the health insurance industry has been inefficient in the provision of health insurance because of increased claims handling and selling costs, and inefficiency in the consumption of health insurance because of consumer befuddlement. If it is true that group health insurance is "bought" rather than "sold," then the buyer and seller are sophisticated enough so that the competitive process should bring about efficiencies and presumably buyers would buy only from the most efficient insurer becuase that is who will be able to offer the lowest price for the policy desired. The profits profile for group insurance, at least during the last few years, seems to indicate that competitive pressures would lead the commercial companies to cut administrative costs. On the other hand, profits on individual insurance have remained positive, which leads one to suspect that this area of health insurance is less competitive, possibly because the buyer of that insurance is less sophisticated. Administrative costs are higher for this form of health insurance than for any other form and charges have been made that they are excessive.[12] The insurance companies claim that it is costly to seek out individuals, sell them insurance, and handle their claims. This is no doubt true. But one may wonder at the difficulties of choice which the individual consumer faces when confronted with a number of policies, each with a differing benefit structure, with different prices from different companies.[13] Because of the large amount of product differentiation on the part of the commercial companies, the consumer may become less price conscious, because he has no common unit of comparison. This makes it possible for the insurers to have less pressure to keep administrative costs low and they have more room for inefficiency. Suppose there is a lack of price competition in a market. If the price is above the competitive price and the firms do not compete in price, they will resort to non-price competition. In general, the non-price competition will be at least partially offsetting, i.e., the change in the "product" will elicit a slightly higher demand price, but a much higher supply price or cost increase. This is one form that a waste of resources can take. It is true that profits can be driven to the competitive level, but only by wasteful expenditures on these non-price variables. Product differentiation is a prime example of a non-price variable that can be used too extensively.

Finally, it must be noted that the payment of the claim itself moves through a number of steps whose costs are not included in the administrative costs outlined above. From society's point of view, these are costs which someone must bear. For most bills, when there is non-assignment,[m] the provider bills the patient and the patient supplies the provider with a partially filled-out insurance claim form. The provider completes the claim form and returns it to the patient, who, in turn submits it to his insurance company. The insurance company pays the patient and the patient pays the provider. The final payment of the bill involves six separate steps, each with its own costs, which are not counted as part of administrative costs.

Notes

1. "Loss of income" also includes payments for accidental death and dismemberment protection. See Health Insurance Institute, *1972-73 Source Book of Health Insurance Data* (New York: Health Insurance Institute, 1972), p. 40.

2. The National Underwriter Company, *1972 Argus Chart of Health Insurance* (Cincinnati: The National Underwriter Company, 1972).

3. For a full analysis of these proposals, cf. Saul Waldman, "National Health Insurance Proposals: Provisions of Bills Introduced in the 93rd Congress as of October 1973," USDHEW, Social Security Administration, Office of Research and Statistics, DHEW Pub. No. SSA 74-11916.

4. As will be apparent, we have benefited from an earlier study and have adopted a model employed therein. See D.B. Houston and R.M. Simon "Economies of Scale in Financial Institutions: A Study in Life Insurance," *Econometrica* 38 (November 1970):856-864.

5. It is clear to the casual observer that product differentiation exists in health insurance policies. An interesting application of the hedonic price index could be made in this industry. This would help decide whether the market functions smoothly enough to explain price differences by product differentiation. There is some structural evidence that the requisite competitive pressures exist, *viz.*, the Herfindahl index was a relatively low 0.03 in 1968. Cf. R. Blair, J. Jackson, and R. Vogel, "Permanent Concentration in Health Insurance," unpublished manuscript, 1973.

6. The National Underwriter Company, *1971 Argus Chart of Health Insurance*, Seventy Third Annual Edition (Cincinnati: The National Underwriter Company, 1971).

7. It has been shown that wide differentials exist ih price for similar basic life insurance packages, that consumers are ignorant of these differentials, and that the life insurance companies are opposed to any form of "unit pricing," cf., Joseph M. Belth, "Statement on Price Competition in the Life Insurance Market," Subcommittee on Antitrust and Monopoly of the U.S. Senate Committee on the Judiciary, February, 1973.

[m]Assignment means that the provider bills the insurance company directly. One might argue that the administrative costs associated with non-assignment are reflected in lower premiums.

8. See the "Statement" of Leonard Woodcock, President, United Auto Workers, before the Antitrust and Monopoly Subcommittee of the Judiciary Committee of the United States Senate, May 11, 1972.

9. See Martin S. Feldstein, "Hospital Cost Inflation: A Study of Nonprofit Price Dynamics," *American Economic Review*, December 1971, pp. 853-873. Martin S. Feldstein, *The Rising Cost of Hospital Care* (Washington: Information Resources Press, 1971). Martin S. Feldstein, "The Rising Price of Physician's Services," *Review of Economics and Statistics*, May 1970, pp. 121-133. Victor R. Fuchs, "The Basic Forces Influencing the Costs of Medical Care," in National Conference on Medical Costs, Washington, D.C., June 27-28, 1967, Report (Washington: U.S. Government Printing Office, 1967), pp. 16-31. Karen Davis, "Theories of Hospital Inflation: Some Empirical Evidence," *Journal of Human Resources*, Spring 1973, pp. 181-201.

10. During the same time period, three other components of the consumer price index, listed by the Bureau of Labor Statistics under "financial and miscellaneous personal expenses," went up at the following average annual rates: (1) bank service charges, checking accounts, 1.8 percent; (2) legal services, short form will, 5.8 percent; (3) funeral expenses, adult, 3.0 percent. Bureau of Labor Statistics, Dept. of Labor, *Handbook of Labor Statistics*, 1972 (Washington, D.C.: U.S. Government Printing Office, 1972), Table 127, p. 293.

11. In fact, since the purchasers of the differentiated product pay the price, one might conclude that the benefits are greater than the costs. But this is too simplistic. To the extent that the market contains imperfections, product differentiation is a non-price variable. Thus, the product differentiation may shift demand less than it shifts costs. The implication is that product differentiation is extended beyond the socially optimal level. If one concurs with Lancaster's theory of product differentiation, one does not need imperfect competition as a prerequisite for product differentiation. See, Kelvin Lancaster, "Change and Innovation in the Technology of Consumption," *American Economic Review*, May 1966, pp. 14-23, and "A New Approach to Consumer Theory," *Journal of Political Economy*, April 1966, pp. 132-157.

12. See the "Statement" of Herbert S. Donenberg, Pennsylvania Insurance Commissioner, before the Antitrust and Monopoly Subcommittee of the Judiciary Committee of the United States Senate, May 11, 1972, pp. 403-414.

13. For an example of this proliferation, see The National Underwriter Company, *Time Saver.* Also in his "Statement" before the Subcommittee on Antitrust and Monopoly (p. 412), Herbert Donenberg pointed out that in Pennsylvania alone in 1971 the state Insurance Department was asked to approve over 6,000 *new* health insurance forms.

3 Blue Cross-Blue Shield[a]

In 1971 Blue Cross had an enrollment of 75,048,794. For the most part the Blue Cross method of payment is "service benefit" rather than "indemnity."[b] The contract that an individual or group receives states the services for which payment will be made in any hospital affiliated with the area plan, regardless of the different hospitals' charges for the services. Payment is made directly to the hospital rather than through the subscriber. Because of this arrangement, Blue Cross usually pays a lower rate per service than do individuals when they pay out of their own pocket or when they pay after having been indemnified by a commercial insurance company. Table 3-1 contains Blue Cross financial data for 1971. As can be seen, there is a relatively wide dispersion in operating expenses. One reason why this variation is present is that the plans are in varying stages in the continual cycle of readjusting their premium levels to account for increases in benefit costs. Also, those plans that provide medical/surgical benefits tend to have higher operating costs than those plans which do not, as indicated by the frequency distribution in Table 3-2.

In 1971, Blue Shield's enrollment was 66,792,721. Member plans are required to write comprehensive Health Care benefit programs which consist of twenty broad benefit areas. Claims are paid by two methods: Payments are made to physicians based upon the usual and customary fees in the regions in which they practice or indemnity payments are made, giving a fixed dollar amount per procedure. Table 3-3 gives financial data for Blue Shield in 1971. As with Blue Cross, the operating expenses of Blue Shield vary widely from plan to plan. Part of this variation is due to the fact that the data for some plans include hospital expenses plus medical/surgical expenses, but even if one excludes these plans, as has been done in Table 3-4, one finds that cost experience varies widely. Blue Shield operating costs as a percentage of subscription income tend to be higher than those of Blue Cross because Blue Shield deals with individual physicians, whereas Blue Cross deals directly with the hospitals.

The aggregate Blue Cross and Blue Shield operations account for some 43 percent of all private health insurance in the United States. In conjunction with

[a]Some of the ideas in this chapter first appeared in Roger D. Blair, Paul B. Ginsburg, and Ronald J. Vogel, "Blue Cross-Blue Shield Administrative Costs: A Study of Non-Profit Health Insurers," *Economic Inquiry*, June 1975. © Western Economic Association.

[b]Service benefit insurance *fully* pays for *specific* hospitals or medical care services rendered. Indemnity insurance, on the other hand, is designed to pay *part* of the cost of services, i.e., a $5 allowance towards the cost of an $8 physician visit or $15 towards the cost of a $25 hospital room.

Table 3-1
Blue Cross Financial Data, January 1, 1971 to December 31, 1971

Plan	Earned subscription income	Claims expense	Operating expense	Percentage of earned subscription income	
				Claims expense	Operating expense
Ala., Birmingham[1]	$123,585,582	$120,569,949	$6,051,164	97.6	4.9
Ariz., Phoenix	25,266,581	25,048,138	1,756,015	99.1	6.9
Ark., Little Rock[1]	37,389,587	35,831,626	2,826,845	95.8	7.6
Calif., Los Angeles[1]	233,019,137	205,773,940	15,377,238	92.3	6.9
Calif., Oakland[2]	174,209,578	168,289,106	14,595,659	96.6	8.4
Colo., Denver	71,915,984	68,986,293	4,348,021	95.9	6.0
Conn., North Haven	134,400,598	127,430,555	5,650,827	94.8	4.2
Del., Wilmington[2]	33,384,120	30,674,677	1,091,816	91.9	3.3
D.C., Washington	98,585,499	93,744,917	5,179,981	95.1	5.3
Fla., Jacksonville	96,390,894	88,449,190	5,445,380	91.8	5.6
Ga., Atlanta	33,282,068	32,721,115	1,683,306	98.3	5.1
Ga., Columbus	25,577,197	23,699,477	1,573,606	92.7	6.2
Idaho, Boise[2]	10,551,622	9,932,771	1,104,475	94.1	10.5
Ill., Chicago	311,925,278	299,234,890	16,601,102	95.9	5.3
Ill., Rockford[1]	8,551,044	7,465,374	935,503	87.3	10.9
Ind., Indianapolis	161,401,559	148,333,927	12,480,910	91.9	7.7
Iowa, Des Moines	55,141,792	53,064,663	3,368,125	96.2	6.1
Iowa, Sioux City	13,951,114	13,101,418	910,278	93.9	6.5
Kan., Topeka	60,430,654	50,973,511	3,692,789	84.4	6.1
Ky., Louisville	71,721,587	66,662,441	3,329,759	92.9	4.6

La., Baton Rouge[1]	38,351,893	34,546,483	3,394,213	90.1	8.9
La., New Orleans	31,075,532	28,538,925	2,205,264	91.8	7.1
Maine, Portland	27,773,198	27,027,376	1,585,783	97.3	5.7
Md., Towson	132,324,775	124,971,003	5,127,392	94.4	3.9
Mass., Boston	320,625,000	305,842,000	11,920,000	95.4	3.7
Mich., Detroit	476,659,000	469,146,000	20,539,000	98.4	4.3
Minn., St. Paul	75,075,494	67,354,396	5,120,086	89.7	6.8
Miss., Jackson[1]	40,860,391	38,668,476	3,396,989	94.6	8.3
Mo., Kansas City	45,612,352	44,439,818	2,631,212	97.4	5.8
Mo., St. Louis	108,124,193	102,347,445	4,703,296	94.7	4.4
Mont., Great Falls[1]	7,629,125	7,195,823	777,142	94.3	10.2
Neb., Omaha	28,542,444	28,648,797	2,351,224	93.4	8.2
N.H., Concord	29,060,338	33,944,451	1,967,935	116.8	6.8
N.J., Newark	294,438,835	274,760,000	11,727,257	93.3	4.0
N.M., Albuquerque	8,404,119	7,843,803	503,850	93.3	6.0
N.Y., Albany	46,187,427	42,948,633	2,390,121	93.0	5.2
N.Y., Buffalo	72,489,257	65,277,806	3,819,522	90.1	5.3
N.Y., Jamestown	2,902,554	2,632,809	127,918	90.7	4.4
N.Y., New York	616,430,071	581,126,820	35,707,304	94.3	5.8
N.Y., Rochester	64,567,341	56,080,114	2,427,184	86.9	3.8
N.Y., Syracuse	35,257,280	33,321,021	1,479,418	94.5	4.2
N.Y., Utica	16,977,305	15,931,957	770,993	93.8	4.5
N.Y., Watertown	2,899,408	2,679,252	221,911	92.4	7.7
North Carolina[1,2]	126,941,000	125,513,000	8,398,000	99.6	6.7
N.D., Fargo	24,418,180	21,465,640	1,311,051	87.9	5.4
Ohio, Canton	18,759,505	17,698,567	587,270	94.3	3.1

Table 3-1 (cont.)

Plan	Earned subscription income	Claims expense	Operating expense	Percentage of earned subscription income	
				Claims expense	Operating expense
Ohio, Cincinnati	138,200,911	125,012,767	5,086,946	90.5	3.7
Ohio, Cleveland	172,187,397	165,857,450	6,592,331	96.3	3.8
Ohio, Columbus	47,747,015	46,999,923	1,646,776	98.4	3.4
Ohio, Lima	9,080,193	8,268,567	273,222	91.1	3.0
Ohio, Toledo	56,378,068	53,880,718	1,910,602	95.6	3.4
Ohio, Youngstown	37,680,808	36,863,573	1,002,408	97.8	2.7
Okla., Tulsa	48,045,231	44,176,293	2,412,014	91.9	5.0
Ore., Portland[1]	48,601,966	44,614,885	3,708,311	91.8	7.6
Pa., Allentown	22,913,843	23,733,790	1,177,869	103.6	5.1
Pa., Harrisburg	61,942,297	59,179,671	2,655,910	95.5	4.3
Pa., Philadelphia	199,841,490	203,623,706	6,985,061	101.9	3.5
Pa., Pittsburgh	199,040,833	185,538,738	9,754,081	93.2	4.0
Pa., Wilkes-Barre	34,412,038	34,539,728	1,233,752	100.4	3.6
R.I., Providence	60,394,190	53,726,867	2,084,063	89.0	3.5
S.C., Columbia	33,239,033	30,875,256	2,042,685	92.9	6.1
Tenn., Chattanooga[1]	92,793,856	89,679,319	6,295,037	96.6	6.8
Tenn., Memphis[1]	20,890,917	19,385,528	1,799,660	92.8	8.6
Tex., Dallas[1]	310,512,435	292,632,278	18,304,225	94.2	5.9
Utah, Salt Lake City	20,750,090	19,550,507	1,249,898	94.2	6.0
Va., Richmond	69,087,564	61,007,145	3,698,193	88.3	5.4
Va., Roanoke	21,024,801	20,552,391	891,977	97.8	3.3
Wash., Seattle[1]	44,226,030	40,022,340	4,398,203	90.5	9.9

W. Va., Bluefield	1,827,077	1,949,051	104,024	106.7	5.7
W. Va., Charleston	14,843,809	15,493,851	675,922	104.4	4.6
W. Va., Parkersburg	3,746,207	3,466,814	107,468	92.5	2.9
W. Va., Wheeling	10,446,063	9,975,025	320,227	95.5	3.1
Wisc., Milwaukee	143,117,526	130,532,111	9,197,055	91.2	6.4
Wyo., Cheyenne	4,988,316	4,461,429	307,511	89.4	6.2
P.R., San Juan[3]	–	–	–	–	–
Total member plans	6,390,126,697	6,053,537,788	338,908,565	94.7	5.3

Notes:

1. Includes medical/surgical plan.
2. Includes reserves for deferred maternity benefits.
3. December 31, 1971 financial report was not received prior to publication.

Table 3-2
Operating Costs as a Percentage of Earned Subscription Income, Blue Cross, 1971

	(1)	(2)	(3)
Percentage of earned subscription income	All plans	Those which include medical-surgical	(1)-(2)
< 2.0			
2-2.9	2		2
3-3.9	15		15
4-4.9	12	1	11
5-5.9	15	1	14
6-6.9	16	3	13
7-7.9	5	3	2
8-8.9	5	4	1
9-9.9	1	1	
> 10.0	3	3	
Totals	74	16	58

Source: Blue Cross-Blue Shield Association, *Blue Cross and Blue Shield Fact Book, 1972* (Chicago: Blue Cross Association and National Association of Blue Shield Plans, 1972).

their obvious importance as private providers of health insurance, the Blues perform much of the administrative work for the Medicare program. Given the large role that the Blues have played (and continue to play) in providing health insurance, it is natural to examine their performance.

Regression Model

As noted in earlier chapters, analysis of administrative costs in health insurance is beset with the problem of variations in output. Different types of insurance policies involve different costs in selling and in processing claims. Even claims processing is far more complex than the mere clerical function since resources are often allocated to policing provider charges and reviewing the appropriateness of utilization. Selling and claims processing costs vary with the nature of the insurance policy and company decisions as to how thoroughly to perform these functions.[c] Thus, variables reflecting variations in type of output must be included to the greatest extent possible. Our present focus on Blue Cross and

[c]It should be noted that an investment of resources in claims auditing brings a return in lower benefit payments, at the expense of higher administrative costs. The next chapter will reveal that the Medicare auditing costs have increased dramatically for this very reason.

Blue Shield plans reduces the potential heterogeneity and serves to clarify the analysis.

The most commonly used measure of operating results in the insurance industry is administrative costs expressed as a percentage of earned subscription income. The primary rationale for this measure is that claims expenses and the administrative costs associated with claims are incurred as premiums are being earned. To avoid tainting the cost function with demand phenomena, however, we use benefits paid plus administrative costs in the denominator instead of premiums earned. We denote this variable OPCOST.[d] In addition to OPCOST, another useful measure is administrative cost per enrollee in the plan (ENCOST). The basic rationale for deflating the administrative costs of various plans by the number of enrollees is that the administrative costs depend more on the number of episodes of service than the number of dollars in a claim. Both of these measures are used as dependent variables in the regression equations. A number of independent variables were entered to capture the effects of variations in output mix. In the Blue Cross equations, a dummy (MEDS) was included to account for the fact that some plans offer medical-surgical coverage as well as hospitalization protection. Medical-surgical bills are smaller, more frequent, and more varied than hospital bills. In addition, the providers are more fragmented. Thus, administrative costs should be higher for the Blue Cross plans that offer this additional coverage.[e]

Another important product mix variable is the proportion of enrollees that are insured through groups (GROUP). The GROUP variable should reduce administrative costs. Similarly, the percentage of claims represented by the Federal Employees Health Benefit Plan (FEHB) should lower administrative costs through efficiencies induced by the homogeneity of policies. Whether hospitals are reimbursed on the basis of charges or costs is included as a dummy variable (CHARGE). We have no hypothesis, however, as to how it should affect administrative costs. Although the operating data do not contain Medicare operating costs and reimbursements, the proportion of total claims represented by Medicare claims (MEDCARE) is known. It is included to reflect the fact that Medicare business should affect costs in the private business through possible economies of scale and/or accounting ploys.

Claims per enrollee (CLE) is entered as this should increase administrative costs. Larger average claim size (ACS) should decrease administrative costs, particularly when the OPCOST variable is used. A final explanatory variable is the proportion of the population in the plan area enrolled in the plan. The larger the proportion, the lower the administrative costs will be. Unfortunately (for

---

[d]The choice of denominator did not affect the results in any appreciable way, i.e., no qualitative conclusion changed. Thus, the analysis is surprisingly robust.

[e]Conversely, for the same reasons, we would expect Blue Shield plans which offer some hospital coverage to have *lower* per unit operating costs than Blue Shield plans which did not offer hospitalization.

Table 3-3
Blue Shield Financial Data, January 1, 1971 to December 31, 1971

Plan	Earned subscription income	Claims expense	Operating expense	Percentage of earned subscription income	
				Claims expense	Operating expense
Ala., Birmingham[1]	$123,585,580	$120,569,950	$6,051,165	97.56	4.90
Ariz., Phoenix	13,142,840	11,585,953	1,946,011	88.15	14.81
Ark., Little Rock[1]	37,389,587	35,831,625	2,826,845	95.83	7.56
Calif., San Francisco[1]	134,726,230	114,290,370	21,682,268	84.83	16.00
Colo., Denver	30,981,639	27,584,728	3,967,039	89.04	12.80
Conn., New Haven[1]	39,420,570	35,483,110	4,030,013	90.01	10.22
Del., Wilmington	13,282,100	11,744,314	1,215,833	89.42	9.15
D.C., Washington	93,739,532	83,574,177	9,707,004	89.16	10.36
Fla., Jacksonville	41,248,775	34,030,703	5,597,757	82.50	13.57
Ga., Atlanta	9,251,465	8,216,169	1,501,439	88.51	16.23
Ga., Columbus	12,808,975	10,808,736	1,932,635	84.38	15.09
Hawaii, Honolulu[1]	42,443,039	40,095,561	2,892,275	94.47	6.81
Idaho, Lewiston[1]	5,684,367	5,104,827	488,615	89.80	8.60
Ill., Chicago	69,000,084	64,043,045	9,414,909	92.82	13.64
Ind., Indianapolis	76,096,793	67,011,306	6,273,129	88.06	8.24
Iowa, Des Moines	46,140,369	47,036,142	5,329,849	101.94	11.55
Kansas, Topeka	33,570,024	30,969,748	3,676,738	92.25	10.95
Ky., Louisville	23,290,299	20,377,912	3,089,185	87.50	13.26
Maine, Portland	8,198,889	7,180,289	1,197,650	87.58	14.61
Md., Baltimore	43,041,143	41,386,941	4,503,728	96.16	10.46

Mass., Boston	116,313,000	103,658,000	13,036,000	89.12	11.21
Mich., Detroit	369,245,819	280,409,333	24,662,768	75.94	6.68
Minn., Minneapolis	41,490,733	34,774,414	6,772,640	83.81	16.32
Miss., Jackson[1]	40,860,391	38,668,476	3,396,989	94.64	8.31
Mo., Kansas City	22,897,334	21,496,845	2,965,723	93.88	12.95
Mo., St. Louis	30,002,568	27,577,988	4,307,795	91.92	14.36
Mont., Helena[1]	9,930,088	9,080,242	1,007,825	91.44	10.15
Neb., Omaha	16,183,798	14,310,679	1,926,122	88.43	11.90
N.H., Concord	16,214,930	16,907,214	2,590,947	104.27	15.98
N.J., Newark	106,103,130	86,952,482	11,848,195	86.86	11.84
N.M., Albuquerque	5,416,105	4,895,170	707,340	90.38	13.06
N.Y., Albany	15,607,179	14,607,389	1,984,041	93.59	12.71
N.Y., Buffalo	38,663,889	37,054,717	4,571,258	95.84	11.82
N.Y., Jamestown	1,458,719	1,184,664	190,677	81.21	13.07
N.Y., New York	135,841,850	124,646,560	21,271,465	91.76	15.66
N.Y., Rochester	23,666,468	21,313,962	1,900,413	90.06	8.03
N.Y., Syracuse	12,663,444	12,859,032	1,494,690	101.54	11.80
N.Y., Utica	7,404,271	7,202,674	909,719	97.28	12.29
N.C., Chapel Hill[1]	126,041,000	126,513,000	8,398,000	99.58	6.63
N.D., Fargo	13,190,028	10,932,782	1,663,052	82.89	12.61
Ohio, Cleveland	44,993,826	40,676,077	4,715,430	90.40	10.48
Ohio, Worthington	83,895,303	75,717,183	10,425,714	90.05	12.43
Okla., Tulsa	19,657,592	18,119,375	2,384,487	92.17	12.13
Ore., Portland	25,131,453	22,575,103	2,534,714	89.83	10.09
Pa., Camp Hill	166,330,890	157,121,640	19,534,926	94.46	11.74

Table 3-3 (cont.)

Plan	Earned subscription income	Claims expense	Operating expense	Percentage of earned subscription income	
				Claims expense	Operating expense
R.I., Providence	21,339,826	20,179,185	2,074,121	94.56	9.72
S.C., Columbia	11,598,477	9,334,565	2,068,655	80.48	17.84
S.D., Sioux Falls	2,317,838	1,682,061	408,555	72.59	17.63
Tenn., Chattanooga[1]	92,793,856	89,679,319	6,295,037	96.64	6.78
Tenn., Memphis[1]	20,890,917	19,386,528	1,799,660	92.79	8.61
Texas, Dallas	40,615,767	38,290,185	5,893,946	89.35	14.51
Utah, Salt Lake City	16,000,129	14,508,379	1,639,680	90.68	10.25
Va., Richmond	32,249,179	28,505,473	3,346,764	88.39	10.38
Va., Roanoke	8,815,949	8,198,469	571,120	93.00	6.48
Wash., Bremerton[1]	5,126,728	4,584,927	459,395	89.43	8.96
Wash., Seattle (KING)[1]	27,479,738	28,503,821	2,615,532	103.73	9.52
Wash., Seattle (WPS)[1]	17,631,979	15,657,987	1,943,289	88.80	11.02
Wash., Spokane[1]	13,900,343	12,830,106	1,354,614	92.30	9.75
Wash., Tacoma[1]	11,622,318	10,950,603	754,090	94.22	6.48
Wash., Walla Walla[1]	637,793	520,346	71,299	81.59	11.18
Wash., Wenatchee[1]	954,657	764,670	121,624	79.05	12.72
W. Va., Bluefield	499,517	472,397	68,400	94.57	13.69
W. Va., Charleston	5,315,061	4,599,634	654,699	86.54	12.32
W. Va., Clarksburg	609,092	542,703	67,979	89.10	11.16
W. Va., Morgantown	448,800	415,853	30,140	92.66	6.72

W. Va., Parkersburg	1,178,250	1,104,819	97,774	93.77	8.30
W. Va., Wheeling	3,367,078	2,910,303	313,477	86.43	9.31
Wis., Madison[1]	44,507,488	39,736,437	4,341,557	89.28	9.75
Wis., Milwaukee	51,522,775	51,940,309	5,409,588	100.81	10.50
Wyo., Cheyenne	2,826,150	2,357,001	356,164	83.40	12.60
P.R., San Juan[1]	19,234,618	17,669,929	1,722,575	91.87	8.98
Total member plans	2,833,730,500	2,548,485,680	287,004,760	89.93	10.48

Note: 1. Includes hospitals.

Table 3-4
Operating Costs as a Percentage of Earned Subscription Income Blue Shield, 1971

Percentage of earned subscription income	(1) All plans	(2) Those which include hospital	(3) (1)-(2)
< 4.9	1	1	
5-6.9	7	4	3
7-8.9	7	4	3
9-10.9	17	7	10
11-12.9	20	3	17
13-14.9	11		11
> 15	8	1	7
Totals	71	20	51

Source: Blue Cross-Blue Shield Association, *Blue Cross-Blue Shield Fact Book, 1972* (Chicago: Blue Cross Association and National Association of Blue Shield Plans, 1972).

our purposes), the variable is clearly endogenous–lower administrative costs should increase enrollment due to a decreased loading factor in the premium. Since the data necessary to estimate an equation for the proportion enrolled were not available, we could not use this variable in the administrative cost equation.[f]

In addition to product mix variables, we want to include variables for firm size and input prices in our cost function. The SIZE variable is the total number of claims paid per plan including both private business and public forms of business such as Medicare, Medicaid, and CHAMPUS.[g] Cost functions were estimated with SIZE and alternatively with SIZE and the square of SIZE (QSIZE). Factor prices are reflected by per capita income in the plan's operating area (CAPY). Unfortunately, wage data were not available.[1]

The data for this chapter were drawn mainly from the *Blue Cross and Blue Shield Fact Book*, 1972, the *Blue Cross Comparative Cost Report*, and the *1971 National Cost Report Statistical Summary* prepared by the National Association of Blue Shield Plans, Finance and Internal Operations Division. The latter two sources are unpublished data, which are confidential and collected internally for plan use. Consequently, the raw data cannot be provided. In this chapter, the

[f]Interestingly, inclusion of the variable did not affect the coefficients of the other variables. It obtained its expected negative sign.

[g]While the focus of our study is on costs in the private business, Medicare and other forms of business could lead to further exploitation of scale economies. We also estimated the equations with the number of private enrollees as the size variable. Surprisingly, the results were not sensitive to the definition used.

individual Blue Cross and Blue Shield plans comprise the observational units. Although the *Fact Book* reports on the operations of seventy-five Blue Cross plans, we could only use sixty-five of them. For Blue Shield, the *Fact Book* reports on the operations of seventy-one plans, but only fifty-six plans could be used for our purposes.

Separate regressions for Blue Cross and Blue Shield plans are estimated in linear and quadratic form. Basically, the same model was estimated for Blue Cross and Blue Shield: The CHARGE variable, however, is deleted from the latter because it is irrelevant and MEDS takes the value of 1 if a Blue Shield plan offers hospitalization and 0 otherwise.

Regression Results

We have presented the regression results for both Blue Cross and Blue Shield in Table 3-5. Since there are two versions of the dependent variable (OPCOST and ENCOST) and SIZE enters alone and along with QSIZE, there are four equations for Blue Cross and four for Blue Shield. In general, the ENCOST equations had better fits than the OPCOST equations. Of course, it does not follow that one measure of costs is superior to the other.[h]

Let us examine the size variables first. When SIZE is entered alone (models 3, 4, 8, 9), no economies of scale are apparent. For Blue Cross, the coefficient simply lacks statistical significance. In the Blue Shield models, however, significant diseconomies of scale are obtained, particularly with ENCOST as the dependent variable. It is interesting that when the QSIZE variable is added (models 1, 2, 6, 7) some of the results change. Since SIZE and QSIZE are highly correlated one must evaluate the *marginal* effect of size on cost. This is obtained by estimating the coefficients in the quadratic cost function and then testing for the significance of $a + 2b$ SIZE, where a is the SIZE coefficient and b is the QSIZE coefficient. It is clear that the *marginal* effect of size varies with the size of the firm in a quadratic cost function. We have presented the size distribution of Blue plans, the calculated marginal effects of size over the appropriate range, and the calculated t statistics in Table 3-6.

For model 1, it can be seen that the marginal effect of size is positive over that part of the range within which most Blue Cross plans are located. The coefficients, however, are not statistically significant at the 95 percent level over any part of the size range. The pattern of scale economies is the same in the ENCOST model (#2) for Blue Cross. We observe diseconomies of scale over the

[h]The simple correlation between ENCOST and OPCOST for Blue Cross is .712; the same correlation for Blue Shield is .001. The equations were also estimated with all size terms omitted to check for multicollinearity. No important effects on the other coefficients occurred. In a search for heteroskedasticity, we regressed the square of the residuals on SIZE and also on QSIZE without detecting any relationships. Since our dependent variable is a ratio, we had no a priori expectation of finding heteroskedasticity.

Table 3-5
Blue Cross and Blue Shield Cost Functions

Model	Dep Var	Constant	Meds	Size	QSize	Group	Medcare
				Blue Cross			
1	OPCOST	.563–01 (1.940)*	.458–01 (8.235)	.818–01 (1.590)	–.154–08 (1.607)	–.430–04 (.160)	.234–03 (1.477)
2	ENCOST	–.239+01 (1.027)	.430+01 (9.618)	.105–02 (2.540)	–.168–06 (2.184)	.280–01 (1.298)	.264–01 (2.072)
3	OPCOST	.571–01 (1.941)	.447–01 (7.978)	.737–06 (.324)		–.827–04 (.305)	.160–03 (1.040)
4	ENCOST	–.230+01 (.955)	.417+01 (9.101)	.237–03 (1.273)		.237–01 (1.065)	.183–01 (1.452)
5	MEDCOST	.175+01 (4.954)		.278–05 (.068)			
6	OPCOST	.188+00 (5.901)	–.473–02 (.396)	–.493–05 (2.785)	.203–09 (3.841)	–.241–03 (.681)	.167–01 (3.975)
				Blue Shield			
7	ENCOST	–.151+00 (.059)	.505+00 (.528)	–.928–04 (.655)	.668–08 (1.577)	.135–01 (.476)	.299+00 (.888)
8	OPCOST	.187+00 (5.174)	–.116–02 (.086)	.139–05 (1.874)		–.348–03 (.866)	.145–01 (3.051)
9	ENCOST	–.156+00 (.060)	.622+00 (.642)	.115–03 (2.167)		.995–02 (.347)	.225+00 (.665)
10	MEDCOST	–.160+01 (.261)		.263–03 (2.104)			

*t is given in parentheses.

range in which most plans operate. In contrast to the results for the OPCOST variable, however, these positive effects of size on average administrative costs *are* statistically significant.

Turning to the Blue Shield models, one finds a dramatic change in the results when QSIZE is added to the OPCOST equation. The explanatory power of the equation is substantially improved and economies of scale appear over most of the range of plan sizes. Presumably, the relationship here is truly U-shaped and the previous linear formulation simply fits it poorly. This pattern does not carry over to the ENCOST model for Blue Shield, where no statistically significant scale effects are obtained.

Results for the product mix variables were for the most part as expected. MEDS is positive in the Blue Cross models, but insignificant in the Blue Shield equations. Its role in the Blue Cross equations appears to be quite substantial.[3] GROUP was not statistically significant in any of the equations. MEDCARE had a positive sign in all models, although it was statistically significant only in models 2, 6, and 8. If Medicare business allowed Blue plans to realize economies of scale, the variable should have a negative sign. The positive sign thus reflects the absence of scale economies and/or the effects of accounting practices.

Charge	CLE	ACS	CAPY	MM	FEHB OPCOST	R^2	Sy
			Blue Cross				
.711–02	–.373–01	–.131–03	.676–06	–.718–01	.428–03	.55	.013
(1.677)	(2.359)	(2.390)	(1.282)	(2.099)	(1.292)		
.168+00	.147+01	–.651–03	.538–04	–.369+01	.171–01	.73	1.022
(.491)	(1.160)	(.210)	(1.269)	(1.344)	(.641)		
.849–02	–.310–01	–.106–03	.696–06	–.756–06	.381–03	.54	.013
(2.002)	(1.994)	(2.952)	(1.300)	(2.185)	(1.137)		
.318+00	.216+01	.213–02	.559–04	–.411+01	.119–01	.71	1.057
(.917)	(1.700)	(.729)	(1.277)	(1.450)	(.434)		
	–.180–04				.173–01	.03	.281
	(1.701)				(.936)		
	–.170–01	–.829–03	–.815–06	–.227–01	.344–01	.50	.019
	(2.632)	(3.355)	(.119)	(1.206)	(1.297)		
			Blue Shield				
	.250+01	.451–01	–.262–03	–.157+01	.228+01	.74	1.550
	(4.835)	(2.279)	(.477)	(1.042)	(1.074)		
	–.111–01	–.546–03	–.679–05	–.133–01	.526–01	.34	.022
	(1.549)	(2.030)	(.893)	(.623)	(1.768)		
	.270+01	.544–01	–.458–03	–.126+01	.288+01	.73	1.575
	(5.282)	(2.836)	(.844)	(.829)	(1.356)		
			(.132–02		.110	.07	4.538
			(.866)		(.469)		

CHARGE reimbursement tended to increase administrative costs in Blue Cross Plans, although the effect approached statistical significance only when OPCOST was used. The effect of average claim size (ACS) depended upon the dependent variable used—a result which is not inconsistent. Similar results were obtained for claims per enrollee (CLE). The presence of federal employee enrollees (FEHB) increased costs, but not to a statistically significant degree. The effect appears to have been more pronounced in the Blue Shield plans. Major medical policies (MM) tended to reduce costs in Blue Cross plans, but not affect them significantly in Blue Shield plans.

Finally, turning to per capita income, this proxy for input prices had positive coefficients in Blue Cross models and negative coefficients in Blue Shield models, but none were statistically significant.

Analysis of the Blue Cross-Blue Shield Results

The results obtained on scale effects are very puzzling in light of our a priori expectations and some previous empirical work. In the previous chapter, we

Table 3-6
Marginal Effect of Size on Average Cost: Models 1 and 6

A. Size Distribution of Blue Plans

Size (Thousands of Claims)	Number of Blue Cross Plans	Number of Blue Shield Plans
0-99	5	7
100-199	8	4
200-299	11	6
300-399	7	2
400-499	6	7
500-599	8	2
600-999	3	6
1000-1999	9	10
2000-2999	5	4
3000-3999	2	1
4000-4999	0	1
5000-9999	1	4
1000-	0	2
Mean Size ($\bar{x}$)	874.4	2136.3

B. Effect of Size

Size	Model 1 Blue Cross OPCOST	Model 2 Blue Cross ENCOST	Model 6 Blue Shield OPCOST	Model 7 Blue Shield ENCOST
$.01\bar{x}$			−6.376−06	−.926−04
			(2.8)	(0.7)
$.05\bar{x}$	.859−05	1.034−03	−6.328−06	−.914−04
	(1.5)*	(2.5)	(2.8)	(0.6)
$.1\bar{x}$	.844−05	1.019−03	−6.267−06	−.900−04
	(1.5)	(2.5)	(2.8)	(0.6)
$.25\bar{x}$	.800−05	.975−03	−6.108−06	−.857−04
	(1.5)	(2.5)	(2.7)	(0.6)
$.5\bar{x}$	.727−05	.902−03	5.828−06	−.786−04
	(1.5)	(2.6)	(2.7)	(0.6)
$\bar{x}$	.581−05	.754−03	−5.267−06	−.643−04
	(1.4)	(2.5)	(2.6)	(0.5)
$2\bar{x}$	.288−05	.460−03	−4.145−06	−.358−04
	(1.0)	(2.2)	(2.3)	(0.3)
$4\bar{x}$	−.296−05	−.129−03	−2.045−06	.213−04
	(0.9)	(0.5)	(1.6)	(0.3)
$8\bar{x}$	−1.466−05	−1.308−03	2.498−06	1.355−04
	(1.4)	(1.8)	(2.9)	(2.5)
$12\bar{x}$	−2.635−05	−2.486−03	7.042−06	2.496−04
	(1.5)	(2.0)	(4.3)	(2.5)

* *t* is given in parentheses.

found decided scale economies for the commercial health insurers. A previous study of life insurance by Houston and Simon also found the presence of scale economies.[4] In addition, one further study with results that are broadly consistent with ours is Hensley's study of financial enterprises.[5] These studies all suffer from a similar shortcoming, *viz.*, that output of the insurance industry appears to be a simple contingency claim, which protects an individual's wealth. There are, however, a host of ancillary services provided by insurers in conjunction with an insurance policy. To the extent that service mix is directly correlated with firm size, specification bias could result. In other words, true economies of scale could be masked by the higher costs that a broader service mix would require. In spite of this problem, the previous studies have found economies of scale to be present.

Initially, one might expect the behavior of the Blues' administrative costs to be similar to that found in the commercial segment of the health insurance industry since many of the services provided are similar. In fact, there would be reason to expect better explanatory power for a cost function for Blue Cross or Blue Shield plans since output among the plans is more homogeneous than among commercial insurers. But the fact that the Blue plans are organized on a private, nonprofit basis may alter these expectations.

Largely due to a belated recognition of their enormous importance in the economy, nonprofit firms have been receiving an increasing amount of recent attention from economists. This has been particularly true in the hospital industry.[6] Many analysts conclude that nonprofit firms have an incentive to achieve technical efficiency, but empirical tests of this conclusion are scarce.

Most studies of nonprofit firms have proceeded by hypothesizing that some objective function other than the profit function is to be maximized. The objective function may include variables such as size of the firm, quality of services, income of those in control, use of capital, and so forth. Maximizing these objectives is often limited by a constraint that the firm break even (including donations and subsidies as revenue). It can be deduced from these models that the nonprofit firm has an incentive to achieve technical efficiency in order to maximize its objectives. Except for those models that include inputs in the objective function, there is also an incentive to achieve input efficiency. Consequently, differences in performance between for-profit and nonprofit firms involve only pricing, the size of the output, and the mix of services that comprise output.

These implications appear to be at odds with popular notions that nonprofit firms are characterized by inefficiency.[7] Assuming that these lay perceptions of nonprofit behavior should be taken seriously, an attempt to reconcile these perceptions appears necessary. Two approaches seem to be plausible. First, one may retain a maximization model similar to those appearing in the literature and include managerial slack as an explicit argument in the objective function. In addition to direct amenities such as plush office space and extensive travel budgets, demanding less than full potential output from a set of inputs makes life more pleasant for many managers. Managerial slack can be traded off against other firm objectives and the maximization model can yield hypotheses regarding what factors will lead to changes in this slack.[8]

Alternatively, one may argue that simple maximization models may not be appropriate for analysis. Decision-making in most nonprofit firms is the outcome of a group process rather than an individual responsibility. Power is often shared among a board of trustees composed of diverse individuals, the professional managers, and, in the case of the hospital, the medical staff. Arrow has demonstrated that decision-making by a democracy of rational individuals need not be transitive.[9] Another problem is that the objectives of nonprofit firms may be somewhat ambiguous. Most of the economic models of nonprofit firms include multiple objectives in the maximization function. Communication of the large amount of information contained in such a function may be exceedingly difficult. Managers may lack clear guidelines while their superiors lack clear criteria upon which to evaluate them. Problems in group decision-making and difficulties in communicating and enforcing institutional objectives throughout the hierarchy are bases for inefficiency that are not handled well by maximization models. Presumably, analyses emphasizing organizational characteristics could deal with these problems.[10]

The preceding discussion can be related to the organizational behavior of Blue Cross and Blue Shield plans. One might imagine some of the objectives of these organizations to be the maximization of insurance benefits in force and of the ancillary services connected with these contingency claims. A preference for managerial slack can be combined with these objectives and a maximization model constructed. The publicly stated objectives of the Blue plans are often highly ambiguous, e.g., community service, and managers can probably interpret them in a fashion favorable to their own individual ends. This ambiguity in objectives may be caused by the diverse composition of some of their governing boards as well as public relations concerns. Apparently, there exist ample opportunities for inefficiency due to managerial slack and to imperfect control creeping into Blue Cross and Blue Shield plans.

Since Blue plans are in competition with commercial insurers in the sale of health insurance, the extent to which managerial slack could develop would appear to be limited. Blue plans, however, enjoy very substantial competitive advantages. For example, state governments often collect a premium tax on insurance sales, but the Blue plans are exempt from these taxes.[i] Exemptions from local property taxes and corporate income taxes are important also. Moreover, Blue Cross enjoys an advantage in the purchase of hospital care for its beneficiaries. These plans reimburse the hospital charges, which are usually

[i]A complete analysis of the tax exemptions that the Blues enjoy would be of great interest. A start has been made: the National Association of Insurance Commissioners (Milwaukee, Wisconsin) keeps a current listing of insurance premium tax rates applicable to health insurers. But much more needs to be done.

higher. Although Blue Shield plans do not have this advantage over their competition in purchasing physician services, they may have an advantage in combating fraud on the part of the physicians through the cooperation of local medical establishments. Given the significant competitive advantages of the Blue plans over commercial insurers, it is possible for administrative slack to be enjoyed by the Blues at the same time they are maintaining or even increasing their market shares.

The possibility of inefficiency or managerial slack in the Blue operations poses important difficulties for the estimation of cost functions. This stems from the fact that the Blue plans may not be operating on the minimum average cost function. These deviations may be both systematic and non-systematic. The low-cost units may decide to permit greater losses through slack than high-cost units (both competition and the maximization of an objective function as discussed above would dictate this). Any systematic deviation from the minimum average cost function could make it impossible to estimate meaningful cost functions because the cross-section observations would not trace out the cost envelope. Non-systematic deviations may result from local competitive conditions, organizational differences, and variations in the objective function from plan to plan. These deviations would serve to reduce the efficiency of estimation. Thus, despite the fact that more homogeneous outputs among the Blue plans would lead one to expect better estimation for the Blues than for commercial health insurers, the nonprofit organization of the Blues works in the other direction and could cause less successful estimation for the Blues.

Reviewing the results actually obtained on scale effects, there is substantial evidence that the Blue plans are *not* operating on their minimum average cost curve. The results of studies of other insurers led us to expect economies of scale, but except for the OPCOST estimates for Blue Shield, these scale economies are not observed. The fact that scale economies show up in a Blue Shield equation rather than one for Blue Cross is consistent with our model. Since Blue Cross plans have more competitive advantages and, thus, can depart more radically from technical efficiency without going out of business, one should expect the observed result. While the evidence is certainly not categorical, we interpret these observed size effects as being consistent with substantial inefficiency among Blue plans, with potential savings from competitive advantages or scale economies dissipated in the form of administrative slack.[j]

The inference that the Blues are enjoying managerial slack is somewhat alarming. Thus, we could not content ourselves with a single test in light of these results. In an effort to reject this inference, we examined two further aspects of

[j]While misspecification resulting from incomplete adjustment for output variation is a possibility, the omitted variable would have to correlate with size to bias the estimate of economies of scale. There is no evidence that this is the case. Similarly, the results of economies of scale among commercial insurers could have resulted from specification bias, but there is no evidence that large commercial insurers tend to have a less expensive output mix than the smaller firms.

Blue Cross-Blue Shield. First, we shall examine the costs that each incurs acting as an Intermediary or as a Carrier[k] for the Medicare program. Second, we shall investigate the potential efficiencies of merging Blue Cross and Blue Shield when the two plans operate separately in a single area.

Blue Cross-Blue Shield and Medicare

As indicated above, the Blues perform many administrative functions on behalf of the Medicare program in their roles of intermediaries and carriers. In performing these functions, the Blues incur additional administrative costs. A comparison of these costs with those incurred in the private segment of the Blues' business can yield much useful information. In particular, we expect to find additional evidence relevant to the behavior of costs. After pouring over the extensive "Principles of Reimbursement for Administrative Costs,"[11] one gets the impression that these rules encourage uniformity in billing for intermediary services. Generally, the intermediaries and carriers are reimbursed on the basis of costs, but the regulations clearly stipulate that *reasonable* costs are those that conform to costs throughout the industry with appropriate adjustments for location, size of firm and other factors. To the extent that the Medicare auditors apply the "reasonable costs" criterion (or threaten to) and have an idea of the "true" cost function, Medicare administrative costs should be substantially uniform after adjusting for size and location. If the earlier inference that substantial managerial slack characterizes the operations of Blue Cross and Blue Shield is correct, the administrative costs of the Blues' private insurance business should not correlate well with the costs incurred on behalf of Medicare. Furthermore, one should expect the variance in private costs to be greater than the variance in the Medicare costs. In order to examine this relationship, Medicare operating costs as a percentage of Medicare operating costs plus Medicare claims costs (MEDCOST) was regressed on OPCOST, SIZE, and CAPY for both Blue Cross and Blue Shield.[12] The results are shown as models 5 and 10 in Table 3-5.[l] There is virtually no relationship between administrative costs in private Blue Business and Medicare business. It should also be noted that the variance of OPCOST is 46 times the variance of MEDCOST. While a more heterogeneous product mix underlying OPCOST may account for part of this, it is unlikely that it accounts for all.[m] Thus, this aspect of the Blue Cross-Blue Shield operation

[k]*An Intermediary* under Medicare is a health insurer that performs much of the administrative function connected with Part A of the Medicare program. A carrier does the same for Part B. For an extended discussion, see the next chapter.

[l]For purposes of this comparison, all sixty-five previously used Blue Cross plans were used because they are all Intermediaries under Medicare. Of the fifty-six Blue Shield plans previously used, only 28 were Medicare Carriers.

[m]To account for the possibility that product mix caused the divergence in operating cost, the residuals of models 2 and 9 in Table 3-5 were run against MEDCOST. Since the two equations contain the product-mix variable MEDS, running the residuals of the equations against MEDCOST, in effect, holds product mix constant. Despite holding product mix constant, the null hypothesis could not be rejected.

does not refute the previous inference regarding the existence of managerial slack and the attendant inefficiencies.

Blue Cross-Blue Shield Mergers

Another topic of interest regarding the administrative costs of the Blues is the extent to which differing organizational structures affect levels of operating costs. There are four types of administrative relationships among Blue plans. In some areas Blue Cross and Blue Shield are operated as one corporation and thus are completely merged. More common is a situation where there are two corporations, but one chief executive and one management team. In our analysis, we consider this form of organization as merged. The most common relationship is one where Blue Cross and Blue Shield have separate corporations and chief executives, but cooperate in some matters, such as sharing a computer. Finally, some plans have no relationship. The latter two arrangements are considered unmerged in our analysis.

A priori, there is reason to believe that the joint Blue Cross-Blue Shield operations would be the most efficient because the merged organizations should have diminished overhead costs. Instead of the need for two sets of executives, only one set would be necessary; and economies of scale in computerized clerical functions could be achieved. Much duplication, such as that in advertising, could be eliminated.[n]

In order to assess the effects of mergers on costs, we combine data on the Blue Cross and Blue Shield plans in an area.[o] Cost functions similar to those in Table 3-5 were estimated with a dummy variable indicating whether or not the plans were effectively merged. As shown in Table 3-7, merged plans had significantly lower costs. Using the OPCOST variable, merging reduced costs by 20 percent at the mean. With ENCOST, the reduction is 26 percent. These empirical results are consistent with a priori reasoning about efficiencies of having only one Blue operation in an area.

If results such as these were presented for firms characterized by profit maximizing objectives, skepticism would be justified. When the cost savings available from merging are so large, one should expect the merged organizational structure to be dominant among profit maximizers. To the extent that the cost differential pointed out is correct, the neglected efficiency of merger lends support to our theory of nonprofit firms. Among nonprofit firms, reasons for *not* merging are plentiful. Lack of competitive pressure from other firms often removes the incentive for merger. Thus, unless one of the plans were faced with serious financial difficulties, there may be little incentive to merge. But possibly

[n]Those areas where one of the Blues did not have a plan were omitted. Nonetheless, sixty-six observations remained.

[o]Karen Davis has pointed out to us that the customers of a merged Blue Cross-Blue Shield would probably receive more *balanced* health insurance protection, and this would eliminate some of the cost inflation pressure on the hospitals and also bring about a more efficient allocation of health care resources.

Table 3-7
Effects of Merger on Combined Costs

Dep Var	Constant	Merge	Size	QSize	Group	FEHB
OPCOST	.885–01 (3.543)*	–.145–01 (3.248)	–.400–05 (3.410)	.156–09 (4.086)	–.318–01 (1.256)	.396–01 (1.853)
ENCOST	–.549 (.216)	–.135–01 (2.968)	–.249–03 (2.081)	.107–07 (2.748)	.250+01 (.969)	.124+01 (.570)

*t is given in parentheses.

of more importance, however, is the fact that transfers of stock, cash, and other assets among corporations to effect a merger cannot be used in a nonprofit setting because there are no stockholders. At the same time, each board of directors would tend to lose members and power. The same would happen to executives. Fundamentally, there may be few ways to compensate those who lose positions of power and influence.[13]

Administrative Costs Over Time

Table 3-8 indicates the changes in Blue Cross' subscription income, claims expense, and operating expenses per subscriber over time. During the twelve-year period, operating expenses per subscriber have gone up at a more rapid rate than either subscription income or claims incurred. This phenomenon is due to the post-Medicare period; between 1960-1966 administrative costs rose 50 percent, while subscription income and claims incurred only increased 75.5 percent and 76.1 percent, respectively. Figure 3-1 indicates the relative movement of these three indices over time. It is difficult to explain why operating costs per enrollee have behaved as they have over time. Claims expenses and subscription income are largely a function of hospital care costs. If hospital costs are increasing at a rapid rate, one would expect claims expenses to increase at an equally rapid rate. Because one of Blue Cross' objectives as a nonprofit insurer is to break even, one would expect subscription income to increase at as rapid a rate as hospital costs and claims expenses. But operating costs per enrollee are a function of a number of variables: the intensity and quality of claims review, the number of claims processed, the size of the claims, the size distribution of those claims, the type of insurance offered (differing deductibles and coinsurance rates), selling costs, more subscriber services offered, equal (women's) rights pressures, and unionization pressures. It would be interesting to know which of these variables has had any significant influence on Blue Cross-Blue Shield operating expenses over time. Unfortunately, the empirical data necessary for estimating the importance of each variable are not yet available.

Medcare	Charge	CLE	ACS	CAPY	MM	$\bar{R}^2$	Sy
.178–01 (3.175)	.984–02 (2.278)	–.826–03 (.213)	–.107–03 (2.755)	.641–05 (1.193)	–.100–00 (1.447)	.53	.014
.122+01 (2.131)	.153–01 (.035)	.221+01 (5.586)	.108–01 (2.732)	.272–03 (.497)	.263+01 (.374)	.74	1.510

Table 3-9 and Figure 3-2 indicates changes in Blue Shield subscription income, claims expenses and operating cost on a per enrollee basis over time. As was the case for Blue Cross, operating costs per enrollee increased at a more rapid rate in the post-Medicare period, and at an even more rapid rate than subscription income or claims expenses.

Conclusions

In this chapter, we have examined separately the average administrative costs of Blue Cross and Blue Shield. The results we obtained can be interpreted in two ways. The failure to associate any variables other than product mix with average administrative costs can be seen as resulting from omitted variables or to lack of incentive to minimize costs as a result of the Blue's nonprofit form of organization. The latter explanation appears more likely when economies of scale found in other studies are considered. The tentative nature of this conclusion would be disquieting in the absence of any other corroborating evidence. But such evidence exists in two forms. First, we have seen that close government monitoring in services purchased from the Blues appears to have reduced the variance in costs. While it is not clear whether this uniformity is at a high or low level of cost, it is suggestive. Second, our analysis of alternative Blue Cross-Blue Shield organizations indicates that opportunities for significant cost savings through merged operations have been eschewed.

The evidence, though somewhat circumstantial, leads one to the conclusion that Blue Cross and Blue Shield have not taken advantage of potential economies of scale to reduce the cost of health insurance. Instead, they have dissipated the potential savings in increased administrative costs.

Notes

1. It might have been desirable to include in our model an average salary independent variable for each plan, but the only direct data available were the

Table 3-8
Blue Cross Earned Subscription Income, Claims Expenses, and Operating Expenses, 1960-71

Year	Total membership	Earned subscription income	Claims expenses	Operating expenses	Subscription income per enrollee (2)+(1)	Claims expenses per enrollee (2)+(1)	Operating expenses per enrollee (4)±(1)	Index of (5) value for year average value 1959-1961	Index of (6) value for year average value 1959-1961	Index of (7) value for year average value 1959-1961
1960	56,063,215	$1,783,171,775	$1,654,950,707	$ 90,821,460	$31.81	$29.52	$1.62	99.4	99.1	98.2
1961	46,489,259	2,011,062,021	1,672,939,270	99,269,193	35.60	33.16	1.76	111.2	111.3	106.7
1962	58,133,290	2,230,746,678	2,103,084,016	107,204,244	38.37	36.18	1.84	119.9	121.4	111.5
1963	59,141,262	2,467,195,398	2,343,231,454	115,227,532	41.72	39.62	1.95	130.3	133.0	118.2
1964	60,615,595	2,731,380,397	2,624,302,497	124,968,615	45.06	43.29	2.06	140.8	145.3	124.8
1965	62,023,856	3,031,470,455	2,887,186,931	134,558,698	48.88	46.55	2.17	152.7	156.2	131.5
1966	63,713,722	3,127,014,039	2,917,963,397	154,773,063	49.08	45.80	2.43	153.3	153.7	147.3
1967	65,725,855	3,276,435,234	3,002,364,075	178,370,328	49.85	45.68	2.71	155.7	153.3	164.2
1968	68,517,832	3,719,627,981	3,578,577,688	212,621,420	54.29	52.23	3.10	169.9	175.3	187.9
1969	71,090,355	4,419,292,095	4,322,338,717	256,227,006	62.16	60.80	3.60	194.2	204.0	318.2
1970	73,535,201	5,385,835,283	5,219,441,358	302,462,973	73.24	70.98	4.11	228.8	238.2	249.1
1971	75,048,794	6,390,126,697	6,053,537,788	338,909,565	85.15	80.66	4.52	266.0	270.7	273.9
				Percentage change						
1960-71		258.4	265.8	273.2	167.7	173.2	179.0			
1966-69		75.4	76.3	70.4	54.3	55.1	50.0			
1966-71		104.4	107.5	119.0	73.5	76.1	86.0			

Source: Columns 1-4 from Blue Cross-Blue Shield Association, *Blue Cross and Blue Shield Fact Book 1972* (Chicago: Blue Cross Association and National Association of Blue Shield Plans, 1972). Columns 5-10 computed from figures contained in mentioned source.

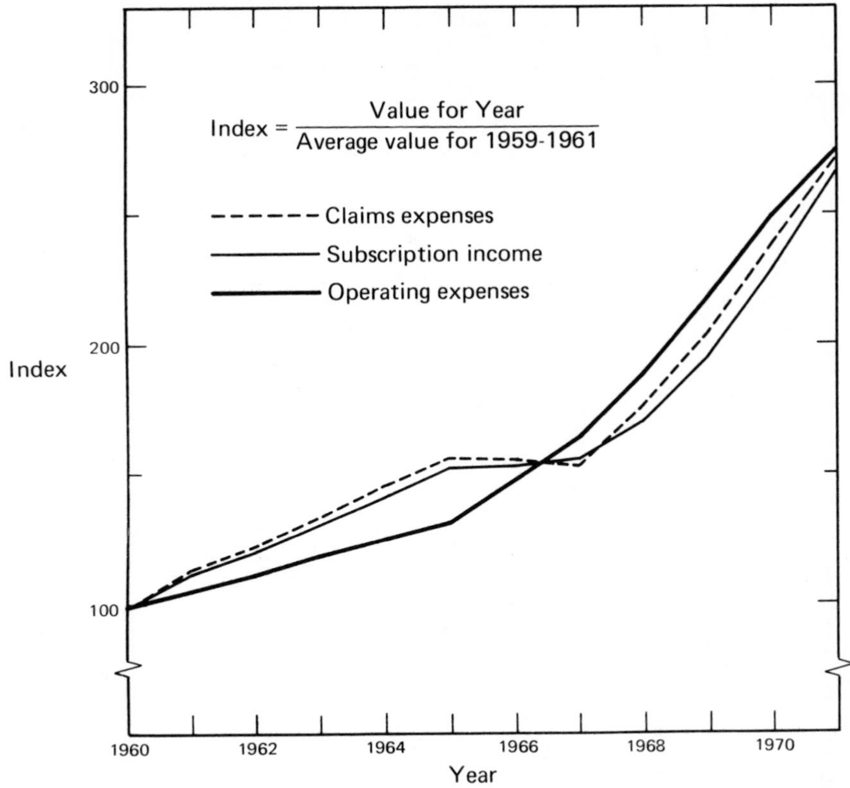

Figure 3-1. Index of Subscription Income, Claims Expenses, and Operating Expenses, Per Enrollee, Blue Cross, 1960-71

salaries that the plans paid to their Medicare personnel. Medicare personnel salaries are higher than regular business personnel salaries because of the necessity of the audit function under Medicare. Medicare auditors earn more because they are more highly skilled than the average employee. Furthermore, arguments have been made to the effect that salary levels are endogenous to the non-profit firm (see, M.S. Feldstein, *The Rising Cost of Hospital Care*, Washington, 1971, and Karen Davis, "Theories of Hospital Inflation: Some Empirical Evidence," *Journal of Human Resources*, Spring, 1973, pp. 181-201). Nonetheless, Medicare salaries were inserted into the model, but the salary variable proved to be insignificant. The U.S. Department of Labor (U.S. Department of Labor, *Handbook of Labor Statistics, 1972*, Washington, 1973) provides an index of average weekly or hourly earnings for selected occupational groups in

Table 3-9
Blue Shield Earned Subscription Income, Claims Expenses, and Operating Expenses, 1960-71

Year	Total membership	Earned subscription income	Claims expenses	Operating expenses	Subscription income per enrollee (2)+(1)	Claims expenses per enrollee (3)+(1)	Operating expenses per enrollee (4)+(1)	Index of (5) value for year average value 1959-1961	Index of (6) value for year average value 1959-1961	Index of (7) value for year average value 1959-1961
1960	44,492,603	$ 741,164,152	$ 670,776,230	$ 76,244,736	$16.66	$15.08	$1.71	98.4	98.8	100.0
1961	46,325,554	837,772,845	752,695,184	82,740,697	18.08	16.25	1.79	106.8	106.5	104.7
1962	48,073,019	974,085,675	868,816,031	91,136,349	20.26	18.07	1.90	119.7	118.4	111.1
1963	49,486,734	1,086,355,622	977,142,095	99,662,095	21.95	19.75	2.01	129.7	129.4	117.5
1964	51,356,864	1,209,394,139	1,095,713,474	108,690,625	23.55	21.34	2.12	139.1	139.3	124.0
1965	52,798,117	1,318,914,790	1,190,485,506	115,940,449	24.98	22.55	2.20	147.5	147.8	128.7
1966	54,627,902	1,396,713,859	1,231,425,788	130,547,403	25.57	22.54	2.39	151.0	147.7	139.8
1967	57,151,382	1,496,266,968	1,268,018,421	149,373,186	26.18	22.19	2.61	154.6	145.4	152.6
1968	60,371,013	1,716,691,657	1,487,940,445	180,900,665	28.44	24.65	3.00	168.0	161.5	175.4
1969	63,471,684	2,028,979,211	1,854,147,845	224,621,757	31.97	29.21	3.54	188.8	191.4	207.0
1970	65,530,827	2,333,474,082	2,176,832,438	255,989,539	35.61	33.22	3.91	210.8	217.7	228.7
1971	66,792,721	2,833,730,500	2,548,495,600	297,004,700	42.43	38.16	4.45	250.6	250.1	260.2
				Percentage change						
1960-71		282.3	279.9	289.5	154.7	153.1	160.2			
1960-66		88.4	83.6	71.2	53.5	49.5	59.8			
1966-71		102.9	107.5	127.5	65.9	69.3	86.2			

Source: Columns 1-4, from Blue Cross-Blue Shield Association, *Blue Cross and Blue Shield Fact Book, 1972*, (Chicago: Blue Cross Association and National Association of Blue Shield Plans, 1972). Columns 5-10 were computed from the mentioned source.

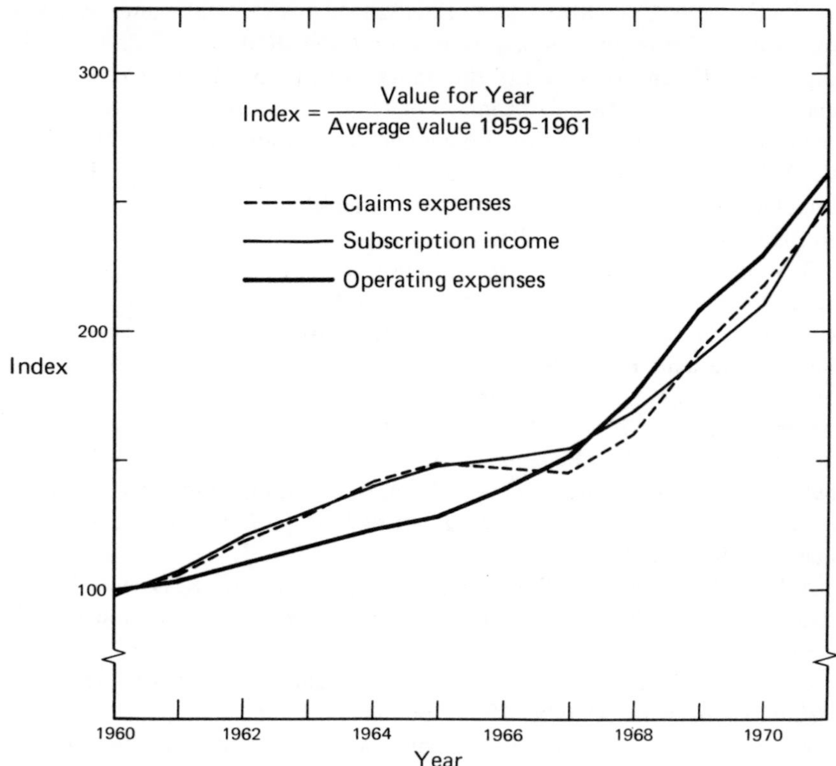

Figure 3-2. Index of Subscription Income, Claims Expenses, and Operating Expenses, Per Enrollee, Blue Shield, 1960-71

metropolitan areas. The data for office-clerical personnel for thirty-nine Blue Cross and thirty-five Blue Shield plans located in metropolitan areas were used. Regression results indicate no statistical significance for this wage variable.

2. Puerto Rico did not distribute data. The plans in Alabama; Arkansas; Mississippi; North Carolina; Chattanooga, Tennessee; and Memphis, Tennessee, are joint Blue Cross-Blue Shield plans and the accounting data do not break costs down for the separate operations. The *Blue Cross* plans in Chicago, Illinois; Kansas City, Missouri; and Bluefield, West Virginia, did not submit a National Cost Report in 1971. Likewise, the Blue Shield plans in Atlanta, Georgia; Illinois; Kansas City, Missouri; Bremerton, Washington; Seattle, Washington (WPS); Spokane, Washington; Bluefield, West Virginia; and Morgantown, West Virginia, did not submit a *National Cost Report* in 1971.

OPCOST, MEDS, SIZE, and GROUP were taken or derived from the *Fact*

Book, while ENCOST, SIZE, MM, FEHB, MEDCARE, CLE, and ACS were taken or derived from the *National Cost Report.* CHARGE was drawn from a list compiled by Karen Davis of the Brookings Institution. The CAPY data were obtained from the AMA's *Distribution of Physicians in the United States.* The data in the *National Cost Report* also contain data for Medicare, CHAMPUS, and Title XIX in the totals. The Medicare, CHAMPUS and Title XIX data were subtracted out of the totals to obtain these variables since we are only concerned with Blue Cross and Blue Shield private business.

3. Models 1-4 reveal why a recent study showed such poor and misleading results. Weiss et al., used all seventy-five Blue Cross plans except Puerto Rico. They failed to recognize the accounting difficulties inherent in using the six plans that are joint Blue Cross-Blue Shield plans. Moreover, they did not make provision for the ten other plans that include medical-surgical as well as hospital benefits. See R.J. Weiss et al., "Trends in Health Insurance Operating Expenses," *New England Journal of Medicine*, September 1972, 287, pp. 638-642, and the subsequent comment: R.J. Vogel, "Trends in Health Insurance Operating Expenses: Comment," *New England Journal of Medicine*, vol. 288, no. 1, January 5, 1973, p. 55.

4. D.B. Houston and R.M. Simon, "Economies of Scale in Financial Institutions: A Study in Life Insurance," *Econometrica*, 38 (November 1970), pp. 856-864.

5. R.J. Hensley, "Economies of Scale in Financial Enterprises," *Journal of Political Economy*, 66 (October 1958), pp. 389-398.

6. These studies include the following: M.S. Feldstein, *The Rising Cost of Hospital Care* (Washington: Information Resources Press, 1971); M.S. Feldstein, "Hospital Cost Inflation: A Study in Non-Profit Dynamics," *American Economic Review*, 61 (December 1971), pp. 853-872; P.B. Ginsburg, "Capital Investment by Non-Profit Firms: The Voluntary Hospital," M.S.U. Econometrics Workshop Paper 7205, revised June 1973; M.L. Lee, "A Conspicuous Production Theory of Hospital Behavior," *Southern Economic Journal*, 38 (July 1971), pp. 48-58; J. Newhouse, "Toward A Theory of Non-Profit Institutions: An Economic Model of a Hospital," *American Economic Review*, 60 (March 1970), pp. 64-73; and M.V. Pauly and M. Redisch, "The Hospital as a Physician's Cooperative," *American Economic Review*, 63 (March 1973), pp. 87-99.

7. Published remarks on this topic are difficult to find, but the authors perceive the point of view in many discussions among non-economists involved in the health care field. Paul Ginsburg, was involved in the early stages of the Economic Stabilization Program. He informed us of a prevailing opinion that if price controls are to be effective, they will work via increases in productivity. This notion assumes that the institutions need price controls to operate on the efficiency frontier.

8. This approach is quite similar to that taken by Williamson in his work on modern corporations and managerial preferences. Cf., O.E. Williamson, *The*

Economics of Discretionary Behavior: Managerial Objectives in a Theory of the Firm (Englewood Cliffs, N.J.: Prentice-Hall, 1964).

9. Cf., K.J. Arrow, *Social Choice and Individual Values* (New Haven: Yale University Press, 1951).

10. Cyert and March have employed this type of analysis in their study of corporations, Cf., R.M. Cyert and J.G. March, *A Behavioral Theory of the Firm* (Englewood Cliffs, N.J.: Prentice-Hall, 1963).

11. Department of Health, Education and Welfare, Social Security Administration, "Principles of Reimbursement for Intermediaries and Carriers," mimeo, Confidential, 1970.

12. ENCOST could not be used for the comparison because under Medicare, Blue Cross does not have enrollees. The individual is enrolled under Medicare; he uses a hospital and the hospital is reimbursed by Blue Cross because the hospital has agreed to use Blue Cross as its Medicare Intermediary. If the individual chooses another hospital, that hospital may use another type of Intermediary such as a commercial insurer. The source of MEDCOST data is (unpublished) the Bureau of Health Insurance, Social Security Administration, *Analysis of Intermediaries' and Carriers' Administrative Costs, July-June*, Fiscal Year 1972 and Fiscal Year 1971. The data for the two fiscal years were averaged in order to obtain estimates for calendar 1971.

13. Ginsburg and Allen have an extensive discussion of mergers among non-profit hospitals. Cf., P.B. Ginsburg and B.J. Allen, "Statistical Analysis of Hospital Mergers," paper presented to the Econometric Society, New York, December 27-30, 1973.

4 Government as a Provider of Health Insurance

The federal government has been a major provider of health insurance since July 1, 1966 when Titles XVIII and XIX, Medicare and Medicaid, were added to the Social Security Act. Medicare, Part A, covers hospital insurance, which is financed through the payroll tax in the same manner as OASDI benefits. Part B covers supplementary medical insurance, which is jointly financed through the general fund and monthly premium payments deducted from the Social Security checks of the aged. Until 1973, these payments bore a systematic relation to expected expenditures under Part B since the premium was set at one-half the cost of Part B. P.L. 92-603 (1973), however, changed the method of financing Part B: The future rate of increase on the beneficiary shares of premium will be limited to the rate of increase in the amount of old age benefits. General revenues will pay the rest.

Although the federal government is the insurer under Medicare, the major portion of the administration of the program is done by the Intermediaries who administer Part A and Carriers who administer Part B. The eighty-two Intermediaries and forty-eight Carriers are reimbursed for the *reasonable* costs they incur in performing these administrative functions for the government. *Intermediaries* are selected by the Secretary of Health, Education and Welfare (HEW) on the basis of nominations by groups or associations of medical care providers. A member of a provider association, however, may elect to be reimbursed by an Intermediary other than that nominated by his association or may elect to be reimbursed directly by the Social Security Administration. In spite of this variety of options, approximately 90 percent of all payments under Part A are currently made by Blue Cross plans.

Carriers, on the other hand, are selected directly by the Secretary of HEW. With the exception of the benefits for railroad retirees, which are administered by the Travelers Insurance Company, Carriers are assigned administrative responsibility for the services provided in a particular geographic area. Thus, for example, beneficiaries who may be Pennsylvania residents, but visiting Florida, are expected to submit claims to the Florida Carrier for any medical expenses incurred in Florida and to the Pennsylvania Carrier for any medical expenses incurred in Pennsylvania. A patient may deal directly with the Carrier or he may assign his bill for collection to the physician, or other supplier, if the provider is willing to accept assignment. Approximately two-thirds of all Part B bills were assigned in 1971. The percentage of assigned claims, however, has decreased in 1972 and 1973. When there is no assignment, the Medicare enrollee has to pay the difference between what the physician charges and what Medicare pays as an allowable charge.

Intermediaries make payments to hospitals, extended care facilities, and home health agencies for covered items and services on the basis of reasonable cost determinations. They also audit provider accounts to determine the accuracy of Medicare billing, make costs reports and checks for reasonableness of costs, perform claim reviews to check the coverage of services billed and monitor the appropriateness of medical treatment. Carriers determine allowed charges for bills submitted to them by physicians or other suppliers of services and pay 80 percent of the allowed charges after an annual deductible ($50 until January 1, 1973, $60 since that date) has been met. The allowed charges are based on customary charges by the individual provider for the specific service and on prevailing charges in the locality for similar services.

It is commonly acknowledged that the Medicare program is more comprehensive and complex than much of the health insurance coverage provided by the commercial insurers and the Blue Cross-Blue Shield plans. Some of Medicare's significant characteristics are: (1) Legislation requires that Intermediaries make payments for services based on reasonable costs. This is accomplished through the application of reimbursement formulae to cost reports made by providers. A consequence of this payment system is the obligation of Intermediaries to audit providers under the Part A Hospital Insurance program. It is noteworthy that provider audits have proven to be one of the largest expenses in the program, but may be more than offset by reduced benefit payments. Commercial insurers do not have this expense and some of the Blue Cross plans require very limited or no audits in their own business. (2) The Medicare Part B program, in determining payments to physicians and other suppliers, applies reasonable charge criteria involving customary and prevailing charge screens. Very few of the other health insurance programs employ such a sophisticated procedure, and these only since refinement of the concept by Medicare. The reasonable charge screens, however, may have resulted in substantial savings in benefit payments from the trust fund. (3) Because of the magnitude of the Medicare program and the broad coverage available to the aged involving most suppliers of health services, a broad multifaceted system is required if checks are made to protect against program abuse. Such safeguards are not utilized extensively in most private programs. (4) There are also basic differences in coverage; Medicare insures the cost of covered services provided by extended care facilities (ECF) and home health agencies (HHA) and a significant amoung of out-of-hospital physician services and other outpatient services. Both the HHA and ECF bills are costly to process in terms of the ratio of administrative costs to benefits. Some of the other health insurance programs cover a small portion of these costs but none cover all the same services for all enrollees. (5) The Medicare program deals principally with the elderly segment of the population which utilizes substantially more health services than those under age sixty-five. (6) When dealing with beneficiaries age sixty-five and over, forms must be designed that can be easily understood by older people. Detailed yet understandable explanations of all actions taken on their individual claims must be provided and resources must be readily available for extensive personal contacts through Social Security offices, Intermediaries, and Carriers. Many resources must be committed to provide explanations of all aspects of a complex program. (7) The final important feature of the Medicare program is the right of the individual to a limited reconsideration of his claims, and beyond that, a hearing by an independent agency to ensure that the program has been properly administered and the individual's rights protected.

Table 4-1 provides a historical account of the administrative cost experience under Medicare through 1973. These data differ from those administrative cost data usually found in Tables M-7 and M-8 in each month's *Social Security Bulletin.* The data in the *Social Security Bulletins* are from the Treasury and represent trust fund withdrawals "in the year." The data in Table 4-1 are trust fund withdrawals "for the year" in question. From the point of view of economic analysis, the "for the year" concept is superior to the "in the year" concept because the former figures indicate when the *real* transfer of resources occurred. For example, total Medicare administrative costs "in the year" fiscal 1973 were $439 million,[1] while administrative costs "for the year" were $494 million. Thus, while only $439 million was actually withdrawn from the trust fund, real administrative resources worth $494 million were actually consumed in that year. When administrative costs are presented as aggregate sums or as a percentage of program expenditures, Part B supplementary medical insurance (SMI) has proved to be more expensive to administer than Part A hospital insurance (HI). This is not surprising. Under Part B, there was a greater absolute number of claims, 54.0 million versus 17.4 million bills for Part A in 1972, and the average amount claimed is much less in Part B than in Part A. "Claims" are used rather than "bills" as the unit of output because data are collected differently for Part B and Part A by the Bureau of Health Insurance. A "claim" is defined as a request for payment for services rendered to a beneficiary, regardless of the number of suppliers or services involved. A "bill" is a narrower concept in that several bills could be included in a claim.

As shown later in Tables 4-5 and 4-6, between 1968 and 1972 the number of Part A bills grew at an average annual rate of 4.7 percent while the comparable figure for Part B claims was 12.4 percent. There is some evidence that physicians are submitting claims more quickly and frequently in order to assure faster payment by the program. For example, early in the program, a physician might have let a patient's bills accumulate for a month before submitting a claim to Medicare or to the patient; now, he may submit claims weekly or biweekly. Bureau of Health Insurance data indicate that the number of services per claim has diminished over time. Also, 1969 was the year in which a number of states brought Title XIX (Medicaid) into the Title XVIII (Medicare) program. Under the provisions of these two Titles, the states pay the Medicare Part B premiums

Table 4-1
Medicare Trust Fund Expenditures: Amount of Benefit Payments and Administrative Costs, Fiscal Years 1967-73 [Amounts in Millions]

				Administrative costs					
				Total		Intermediaries		Government	
Fiscal year	Number of enrollees (in thousands)	Total expenditures	Benefit payments	Amount	Percentage of expenditures	Amount	Percentage of expenditures	Amount	Percentage of expenditures
					HI and SMI				
1967	19,115	$3,345	$3,171	$174	5.1	$ 94	2.8	$ 80	2.4
1968	19,496	5,376	5,126	250	4.7	153	2.9	97	1.6
1969	19,815	6,603	6,299	304	4.6	193	2.9	110	1.7
1970	20,278	7,133	6,783	350	4.9	234	3.3	116	1.6
1971	20,732	7,885	7,478	407	5.2	263	3.4	144	1.8
1972	21,150	8,793	8,364	429	4.9	285	3.2	145	1.6
1973	21,601	9,534	9,040	494	5.2	310	3.3	184	1.9
					HI				
1967	19,088	$2,583	$2,508	$ 75	2.9	$25	1.0	$49	1.9
1968	19,465	3,832	3,736	96	2.5	41	1.1	54	1.4
1969	19,751	4,768	4,654	114	2.4	56	1.2	57	1.2
1970	20,174	4,940	4,804	136	2.7	73	1.5	63	1.3
1971	20,588	5,591	5,443	148	2.6	74	1.3	74	1.3
1972	20,970	6,279	6,109	170	2.7	90	1.4	79	1.3
1973	21,375	6,843	6,649	194	2.9	87	1.3	107	1.6

					SMI				
1967	17,750	$ 762	$ 663	$ 99	12.4	$ 8	8.5	$31	3.9
1968	18,021	1,545	1,390	155	10.1	112	7.3	43	2.8
1969	18,885	1,835	1,645	190	10.3	137	7.4	53	2.9
1970	19,329	2,193	1,979	214	9.7	161	7.3	53	2.4
1971	19,739	2,294	2,035	259	11.3	190	8.3	69	3.0
1972	20,150	2,514	2,255	259	10.2	195	7.7	65	2.6
1973	20,545	2,691	2,391	300	11.4	223	8.5	77	2.9

Source: Unpublished Department of the Treasury data.

for the aged who are medically indigent. Title XIX encourages a more frequent submission of claims on the part of physicians. In the case of Part A, the Intermediaries deal primarily with the hospitals and the average hospital bill is larger than the average physician bill. SMI, on the other hand, reimburses primarily for the services of individual physicians.

The combined administrative expenses of the Intermediaries and government for Medicare ranged from 4.6 percent to 5.2 percent of expenditures between fiscal 1967 and 1973. As was pointed out earlier, these figures are lower than those for the commercial health insurers and Blue Cross-Blue Shield. One important reason why this particular measure is lower for Medicare is that the aged become ill more frequently than the rest of the population[2] and consequently have larger average annual medical expenditures.[3] If the administrative costs for a large annual medical bill are not much greater than the administrative costs for a smaller annual bill, administrative costs will represent a much larger proportion of the smaller annual bill amount.[4]

Another equally important reason for the lower ratio of Medicare administrative costs to benefits is that the uniformity of the Medicare program makes handling its health insurance product easier than dealing with the multiple benefit packages often offered by the commercials and Blue Cross-Blue Shield. Furthermore, the commercial insurers incur large selling and underwriting costs for individual health insurance.

Table 4-2 contains a more detailed presentation of Medicare's administrative costs by administrative entity for fiscal year 1971. In both HI and SMI, the overwhelming majority of administrative costs are the responsibility of the Social Security Administration. Although the Social Security Administration was responsible for $391.5 million of the HI and SMI obligations in Fiscal 1971, $263.6 million or 67.3 percent of that amount was obligated to the Intermediaries and Carriers who are reimbursed for the mechanics of claims payments, provider audits, utilization/claims reviews and other administrative duties by Social Security at cost. Almost the entire Treasury obligation represents the costs incurred by the Internal Revenue Service in collecting the Medicare portion of the Social Security tax when it collects payroll taxes. The Treasury's costing method consists of a computed unit cost applied to the actual number of FICA tax returns received by IRS. Included in the compound unit cost are the operating and administrative costs incurred by IRS for processing tax returns and remittances, obtaining delinquent returns, collecting delinquent accounts, and auditing employers' records. Because the operations applicable to tax returns affecting the Trust Funds are so closely integrated with non-trust fund matters, the Treasury does not maintain separate cost records for Trust Fund activities. Therefore, percentage factors are used to arrive at a computed cost based upon known activity costs from special studies and from the judgments and experiences of personnel at pertinent organizational levels. This unit cost is adjusted periodically to recognize program changes and other factors such as general pay increases.

Table 4-2
Medicare Administrative Costs (Obligations), Fiscal Year 1971

Agency or program	HI	SMI
Total	$148,731,136	$260,548,845
Department of the Treasury	6,379,468	43,766
Bureau of Accounts	169,082	16,235
Internal Revenue Service	6,210,340	0
Office of the Treasurer of the U.S.	46	9
Secret Service	0	27,522
Civil Service Commission	0	126,281
Department of Health, Education, and Welfare:		
Office of the Secretary	1,507,000	1,487,000
Departmental management	740,000	1,402,000
Office for Civil Rights	767,000	85,000
Community Health Services	3,755,000	764,000
Social Security Administration	135,567,668	256,291,798
Bureau of District Office Operations	11,265,482	20,406,528
Bureau of Retirement and Survivors Insurance	2,095,368	3,141,596
Bureau of Health Insurance	13,664,327	14,742,804
Health insurance State agencies	10,138,000	2,472,000
Intermediaries and carriers	73,877,000	189,723,000
Bureau of Data Processing	19,544,480	18,168,783
Office of Research and Statistics	401,154	3,635,087
Bureau of Hearings and Appeals	1,436,806	—
Incentive reimbursement experimentation[1]	364,000	0
All other	2,781,051	4,002,000
Construction	1,522,000	1,836,000

Source: Unpublished Social Security Administration data.

Note: 1. Authorized under the Social Security Amendments of 1972 and administered by the Bureau of Health Insurance and the Office of Research and Statistics.

The Division of Disbursement of the Bureau of Accounts issues checks for the Trust Funds. Primarily, the cost of issuing checks is based upon (1) direct labor and general supervision which is allocated on the basis of the ratio of time consumed to prepare Trust Fund checks (including the handling of return checks, etc.) to total time expended in preparing all types of checks; (2) the overhead cost of the central office of the Division of Disbursement, which is allocated in a ratio to the direct labor which takes account of the varying complexity of management service activities; (3) rental and depreciation of equipment, which is allocated on the basis of the ratio of usage for Trust Fund checks to total checks; (4) postage and fees based on a count of Trust Fund checks mailed; and (5) all other expenses such as blank checks, travel and supplies, which are allocated on the basis of the ratio of the volume of Trust Fund checks issued to the total volume of checks issued.

Trust Fund accounting records are maintained by the Bureau of Accounts, which also invests their funds and performs the annual audit. The cost of performing these services for the Trust Funds is based upon time consumed and volume of work. Additionally, the Office of the Treasurer of the United States performs (1) payment and reconciliation of U.S. government checks and (2) handles claims arising from the loss, theft, and forgery of such checks. Costs applicable to the Trust Fund are based upon the check volume processed. The percentage derived from the check volume is then applied to the total cost incurred by the Treasurer's Office in performing these two functions.

The U.S. Secret Service investigates forgeries of government checks. Costs applicable to the Trust Fund for this service are based upon the actual number of Trust Fund check forgery cases closed during the fiscal year times the unit cost developed from the total cost incurred by the Secret Service investigating all government check forgeries. Because it makes Medicare Part B premium deductions from Civil Service retirement annuitant checks, the Civil Service Commission also charges the Medicare trust fund. Sixty-four percent of the $126 thousand is for electronic data processing services and the remainder pays for personnel compensation and benefits, supplies, materials, equipment maintenance, and miscellaneous charges.

The heading listed as "Departmental Management" contains charges made to the Trust Fund by the following offices within HEW: Office of the Secretary, Office of the Comptroller, Office of the General Counsel, Office of Community and Field Services, and Office of Administration. Each of the above offices within the Office of the Secretary of HEW estimates the amount of time that its personnel spend on Medicare matters and then the Office of the Secretary bills the Social Security Administration for the amounts of money involved. Section 201(g) of the Social Security Act authorizes the Secretary to transfer Social Security Administration Trust Funds to pay for Office of the Secretary administrative functions related to the SSA program. The amount of the transfer is specified annually in the appropriation law and is determined by the proportion of resources in the Office of the Secretary devoted to Social Security Administration functions. Interpretation of "related administrative function" is strict in order to prevent simple pro rata requisitioning based on SSA's percent of HEW personnel. The strict interpretation encompasses such functions as (1) research efforts related to SSA's programs including health insurance, nursing homes, and income maintenance; (2) congressional liaison directly related to SSA matters; (3) personnel, equal opportunity and management of analytical resources directly related to SSA; (4) legal services rendered to or related to SSA; (5) budget, financial, and audit resources related to SSA; (6) resources expended to secure SSA facilities; and (7) civil rights compliance efforts aimed at provider institutions receiving SSA funds.

The Social Security Act authorizes the federal government to contract with state agencies to carry out certain functions under both the disability insurance and Medicare programs. State agencies certify hospitals, extended care facilities and other providers of medical services for participation in Medicare. In addition, Medicare payments are made to hospitals, extended care facilities, and other providers of services. It is necessary to make periodic reviews to insure that these agencies and institutions comply with the provisions of the Civil Rights Act before receiving payments from the Social Security Trust Fund. Title VI of that Act prohibits the use of federal funds for programs that discriminate on the basis of race, color, or national origin. The Office of Civil Rights conducts these compliance reviews. For example, during fiscal year 1970, the Office of Civil Rights visited approximately 500 hospitals and extended care facilities eligible for Medicare payments, reviewed forms giving statistics on occupancy from some 12,000 hospitals and providers, and conducted 50 reviews of state agencies with responsibility in the Medicare program to determine whether these institutions and agencies were complying with Civil Rights requirements.

The Health Services Administration and Health Resources Administration[a] provide a number of services under the Medicare program. Their basic task, however, is to set standards for providers and suppliers of health care services and to help see that such standards are enforced.

The 1967 and 1972 Social Security amendments provide authorization to conduct experiments for reimbursement of providers of services on a basis other than the "reasonable cost" or "reasonable charges" provisions generally applicable under the Medicare program and for testing the effect of providing additional benefits such as day care and intermediate care. These experiments are implemented in an effort to achieve incentives for economy while maintaining or improving quality in the provision of health services. Costs of administering and evaluating the experiments are distributed currently on an estimated basis between the Hospital Insurance and Supplementary Medicare Insurance Trust Funds. Finally, various units of the Social Security Administration perform Medicare functions, which are largely self-explanatory in Table 4-2.

It is possible to maintain that a small portion of the allocation of costs to Medicare, and between HI and SMI, by various offices involved in its functioning is a rather arbitrary process, especially the allocation of overhead. Most business firms, however, as well as government agencies, face the same problem in allocating costs to a particular product or program. Rules of thumb are usually developed.[b] Educated estimates by key personnel are usually made and strict accounting procedures are followed. At worst, internal competition for funds ought to bring about a reasonable allocation of costs; one manager might protest vigorously if costs were unfairly imputed to his branch of the operation by other branch managers.

---

[a]Formerly the Health Services and Mental Health Administration.

[b]The economist's preferred rule for allocating such costs is to do so on the basis of marginal revenues. It is open to question whether this procedure is approximated by real firms or governments.

One might also argue that Medicare administrative costs are artificially low because the fair rental value of government buildings is not included in Medicare costs and government does not depreciate its capital goods. This is only partially true, because the government does rent some of its office space[c] and these rents are included in the cost of Medicare. Moreover, it must be remembered that the preponderant burden of Medicare administration is borne by the Intermediaries who *do* include rents and depreciation in the costs that they report to the Social Security Administration and for which they are reimbursed. Thus, while it must be conceded that Medicare costs are understated because government rent and depreciation are not included in the costs, the probable amount that is excluded must be negligible compared to all other administrative costs. It has also been suggested that Medicare's true administrative costs are understated because the amount of congressional time spent on hearings, investigations, and legislation pertaining to Medicare are not included in Medicare administrative costs. The authors elected not to attempt such a refinement in the cost computations for two reasons. First, there is no logical place to draw the line. For example, if congressional time were included in Medicare administrative costs, then the time spent by state insurance commissions and by state lawmakers on state laws and regulations pertaining to health insurance ought to be included in the administrative costs of Blue Cross-Blue Shield and the commercial health insurers. Second, it would be impossible, as a practical matter, to compute these costs.

Administrative Costs per Enrollee and per Bill

In addition to the administrative costs to premiums and claims costs ratios already used and discussed, it is also possible to analyze Medicare on a per enrollee and on a per bill basis. Since these two measures are not a function of the size of the denominators, claims costs or premiums, which themselves are a function of the amount of medical care consumed and the price of care, they allow one to view administrative costs within a different perspective.[5]

Table 4-3 contains annual data for the combined HI and SMI programs per enrollee basis and also contains similar data for the HI and SMI programs separately. Table 4-4 also contains the percentage change in each item between 1967 and 1973 and between 1968 and 1973 as well as yearly percentage changes. Benefits per enrollee have increased at a faster rate than administrative expenses per enrollee under both HI and SMI if one uses 1967 as a base year. On a year-to-year basis, however, these changes have been somewhat uneven. The reader will note the large increase in benefits per enrollee and administrative cost per enrollee that occurred between 1967 and 1968, particularly under the SMI

[c]For example, the building in which most of this study was conducted and written is rented by the Social Security Administration from a private firm.

Table 4-3
Medicare Trust Fund-Expenditures: Amount Per Enrollee for Benefit Payments and Administrative Costs, Fiscal Years 1967-73

Type of expenditure	1967	1968	1969	1970	1971	1972	1973
				HI and SMI			
Expenditures per enrollee	$174.97	$275.77	$333.21	$351.74	$380.34	$415.77	$441.37
Benefit payments	165.89	262.93	317.89	334.49	360.69	395.46	418.50
Administrative costs	9.08	12.84	15.32	17.25	19.65	20.31	22.87
Intermediaries and carriers	4.89	7.87	9.76	11.53	12.71	13.46	14.34
Government	4.19	4.97	5.56	5.72	6.94	6.84	8.53
				HI			
Expenditures per enrollee	$135.32	$196.84	$841.39	$244.89	$271.57	$299.42	$320.13
Benefit payments	131.39	191.93	235.64	238.13	264.37	291.32	311.06
Administrative costs	3.93	4.91	5.75	6.76	7.20	8.10	9.07
Intermediaries and carriers	1.35	2.11	2.85	3.63	3.59	4.29	4.06
Government	2.58	2.80	2.90	3.13	3.61	3.81	5.02
				SMI			
Expenditures per enrollee	$42.91	$85.73	$97.33	$113.43	$116.24	$124.79	$130.99
Benefit payments	37.35	77.13	87.25	102.38	103.11	111.91	116.38
Administrative costs	5.56	8.60	10.08	11.05	13.13	12.88	14.61
Intermediaries and carriers	3.81	6.23	7.27	8.30	9.61	9.66	10.86
Government	1.75	2.37	2.81	2.75	3.52	3.22	3.75

Source: Unpublished Social Security Administration data.

Table 4-4
Medicare Trust Fund Expenditures: Percentage Change in Amount Per Enrollee for Benefits Payments and Administrative Costs, Fiscal Years, 1967-73

Type of expenditure	1968	1969	1970	1971	1972	1973	1967-73	1968-73
					HI and SMI			
Expenditures per enrollee	57.6	15.8	5.6	8.1	9.3	6.2	152.3	60.1
Benefit payments	58.5	20.9	5.2	7.8	9.6	5.8	152.4	59.3
Administrative costs	41.4	19.3	12.6	13.9	3.4	12.6	151.8	78.1
Intermediaries and carriers	60.9	24.0	18.1	10.2	5.9	6.5	193.3	82.2
Government	18.6	11.9	2.9	21.3	−1.4	24.7	103.6	71.6
					HI			
Expenditures per enrollee	45.5	22.6	1.4	10.9	10.3	6.9	136.6	62.6
Benefit payments	46.1	22.8	1.1	11.0	10.2	6.8	137.4	62.0
Administrative costs	24.9	17.1	17.6	6.5	12.5	12.0	130.8	84.7
Intermediaries and carriers	56.3	35.1	27.4	−1.1	19.5	−5.4	200.7	92.4
Government	7.7	3.9	7.9	15.3	5.5	31.8	95.3	79.9
					SMI			
Expenditures per enrollee	99.8	13.5	16.5	2.5	7.4	5.0	265.3	52.8
Benefit payments	106.5	13.1	17.3	.7	8.5	4.0	213.5	50.6
Administrative costs	54.7	17.2	9.6	18.8	−1.9	13.4	163.1	70.0
Intermediaries and carriers	63.5	16.7	14.2	15.8	.5	12.4	185.4	74.3
Government	35.6	19.1	−2.5	28.5	−8.8	16.8	115.5	58.9

Source: Unpublished Social Security Administration data.

program. At the outset of the Medicare program there was a considerable lag before bills were submitted and processed for reimbursement. Benefit and administrative cost figures for 1968 reflect much of the catch-up for 1967.[6] Furthermore, Intermediary and Carrier administrative costs per enrollee have increased at a more rapid rate than those of the government, with the cost increase differential being greater under the HI program. Again, though, the largest administrative cost increase per enrollee occurred between 1967 and 1968 for the Intermediaries and Carriers, when the catch-up for 1967 arrived. Since 1968, the annual percentage change in administrative costs per enrollee has been about thirteen percent although it was 19.3 percent between 1968-69 and dropped to 3.4 percent in 1971-72.

The content of Tables 4-3 and 4-4 follow a pattern that one might expect from a large new program such as Medicare: the program is enacted and beneficiaries initially respond slowly and then more rapidly. This pattern is shown by the 1967-68 percentage changes. Annual increases in benefits slow down as the most pressing needs of beneficiaries are met. As claims are submitted with a lag, the administrative mechanism needs time to consolidate itself and then rates of increase in administrative costs also slow down. If one uses 1968 as a base year, one finds that administrative costs per enrollee have been growing at a more rapid rate than benefits per enrollee. Several factors account for the difference in growth rates. One was the aforementioned lag in benefit payment. And, as mounting benefit payments attracted closer congressional scrutiny and executive department interest in cost control, more emphasis was placed upon careful monitoring of provider bills, which reduced the rate of increase in benefit payments. Additional burdens were added to the administrative system by amendments on utilization review, capital controls, and generally more paper work to justify the payment of bills and interim cost payments. These events led quite naturally to an acceleration in the increase in administrative costs and a deceleration in the rate of growth of benefit payments. Since percentage changes over a period of years are a function of both the base year chosen and the terminal year, it is difficult to draw inferences without additional information as to what transpired over time. Evidence will be presented below which shows that monitoring activities have increased considerably. Also, price controls went into effect August 15, 1971. The effect of these controls was to slow the rate of increase of all prices and costs during fiscal 1972.

Table 4-5 contains further data on Intermediary operating statistics between fiscal 1968 and 1972. Comparable data for the Carriers will be analyzed separately because of the difference in the nature of their tasks under Medicare. The largest average annual percentage increases in Table 4-5 are all related to provider audit activity. Between those years, the total number of bills processed increased at an average annual rate of 4.1 percent while total Intermediary administrative costs increased at an average annual rate of 18.7 percent.[d] Even

[d]These administrative costs do not contain any government administrative costs.

Table 4-5
Hospital Insurance Intermediary Operating Statistics, 1968-72

Item	1968	1969	1970	1971	1972	Average annual percentage change, 1968-72
Benefit payments:						
Total amount (in millions)	$3,727	$4,638	$5,017	$5,587	$6,288	14.0
Per bill	$256.72	$301.72	$320.17	$341.51	$361.21	8.9
Administrative costs:						
Total amount (in millions)	$55.4	$75.8	$99.4	$99.9	$110.1	18.7
Provider audit	12.2	22.6	35.6	27.0	31.4	27.0
Other	43.2	53.2	63.8	72.9	78.7	16.2
Per bill	$3.82	$4.93	$6.34	$6.04	$6.33	13.5
Provider audit	.84	1.47	2.27	1.59	1.81	21.0
Other	2.98	3.46	4.07	4.45	4.52	11.0
Average annual salary per employee	([1])	$6,947	$7,671	$8,556	$9,335	10.3[2]
Provider audit	([1])	9,651	10,100	10,379	11,757	6.8[2]
Other	([1])	6,638	7,260	8,128	8,808	9.9[2]
Labor cost per bill	([1])	$2.72	$3.38	$3.57	$4.02	13.9[2]
Without audit	([1])	2.33	2.73	3.01	3.08	9.7[2]
Provider audit	([1])	.39	.65	.56	.94	34.0[2]
Bills processed (in millions)	14.5	15.4	15.7	16.4	17.4	4.7
Per employee (per year)	2,828.04	2,552.73	2,266.64	2,276.68	2,327.44	–4.9
Per employee without audit	3,013.30	2,849.74	2,655.62	2,703.15	2,855.74	–1.3

Average annual manpower (number of persons)	5,134	6,022	6,913	7,186	7,480	9.9
Provider audit	322	618	1,001	1,119	1,387	44.0
Other	4,812	5,404	5,912	6,067	6,093	6.1

Source: Unpublished Social Security Administration data.

Notes: 1. Data not available.
2. Computed for 1969-72.

though provider audit costs peaked at $35.6 million in 1970, they still managed to show an average annual rate of increase of 27.0 percent during the five-year period. Since provider audit costs constituted almost 30 percent of all administrative costs in 1972, it is obvious that emphasis is being placed upon the correctness of hospital cost accounting under Medicare Part A.[e]

Of the $54.7 million increase in total administrative costs during that period, $11.4 million[f] can be attributed to the increased volume of bills, $19.2 million to an increase in audit activity, and the remaining $24.4 million is due to the increased costs of resources allocated to claims. Table 4-5 indicates that the average salary which the Intermediaries paid their employees increased at an average annual rate of 10.3 percent during 1969-72, while employee productivity, declined by 3.2 percent annually during the same period. But a decline in productivity measured in this manner is not without ambiguity. The amount of manpower allocated to provider audit increased at an average annual rate of 44.0 percent. Assuming that this increased audit activity led to more proper cost allocation within the hospitals and thus to more appropriate Medicare reimbursement to the hospitals, it may be one reason why the amount of benefits paid under the program did not increase at an even more rapid rate. Bills processed per employee decreased at an average annual rate of 1.3 percent if provider audit activity is not included. Labor costs per bill have increased at average annual rates of 34.0 percent or 9.7 percent during 1969-72, depending upon whether or not one includes the audit activity.

Table 4-6 contains Part B Carrier operating statistics for the period 1968-72. During those years the number of claims processed increased at an average annual rate of 12.4 percent while benefits paid only increased at an average annual rate of 10.4 percent. As a consequence, benefits per claim actually declined by 1.9 percent per year. Claims processed under Part B have increased at almost two and one-half times the rate of bills processed under Part A over the four year period. Under Part A, benefits have gone up at an average annual rate of 14.0 percent, while under Part B, they have increased at a slower rate, 10.4 percent. This result could have been expected because inflation has been greatest in the hospital sector of the medical care market. As with Part A, administrative costs have increased at a more rapid rate than benefits paid. Administrative costs per claim, however, have remained quite stable during these five years and the number of claims processed per employee has actually increased at an average annual rate of 8.5 percent. The reader will recall that Part A results showed a slight decrease in productivity, measured in this fashion (when provider audit was included). Furthermore, the labor cost per claim

[e]The decrease in provider audit between 1970 and 1972 was due to cost-benefit analyses on the audit function. The decision was made to reduce the number of full audits where appropriate hospital cost allocation had taken place.

[f]This figure is obtained by multiplying the change in the number of bills processed between 1968-72 times the unit cost per bill in 1968.

Table 4-6
Supplementary Medical Insurance Carrier Operating Statistics, 1968-72

Item	1968	1969	1970	1971	1972	Average annual percentage change, 1968-72
Benefit payments:						
Total amount (in millions)	\$1,319	\$1,510	\$1,652	\$1,775	\$1,958	10.4
Per claim	\$39.02	\$39.12	\$37.80	\$36.45	\$36.26	–1.9
Administrative costs:						
Total amount (in millions)	\$99.4	\$118.4	\$138.1	\$159.9	\$171.8	14.7
Per claim	\$2.94	\$3.07	\$3.16	\$3.28	\$3.18	2.0
Average annual salary per employee	([1])	\$6,077	\$6,507	\$7,136	\$7,568	7.6[2]
Labor costs per claim	([1])	\$2.02	\$1.91	\$1.92	\$1.86	–2.8[2]
Claims processed[3] (in millions)	33.8	38.6	43.7	48.7	54.0	12.4
Per employee (per year)	2,940	3,007	3,406	3,710	4,072	8.5
Average annual manpower (number of persons)	11,494	12,836	12,828	13,124	13,259	3.6

Source: Unpublished Social Security Administration data.

Notes: [1] Data not available. [2] Computed for 1969-72. [3] Includes railroad retirement benefits administered by Travelers Insurance Company.

actually dropped 2.8 percent per year between 1969 and 1972 even though average salary went up 7.6 percent annually.

A comparison of Figures 4-1 and 4-2 gives some insight into why Part A and Part B operating statistics differ in rather important respects. The data are graphed on an administrative cost per bill and per claim basis, respectively, and unit costs for the components of administrative costs are presented. Although Part B administrative costs appear to be higher than Part A's when expressed as a

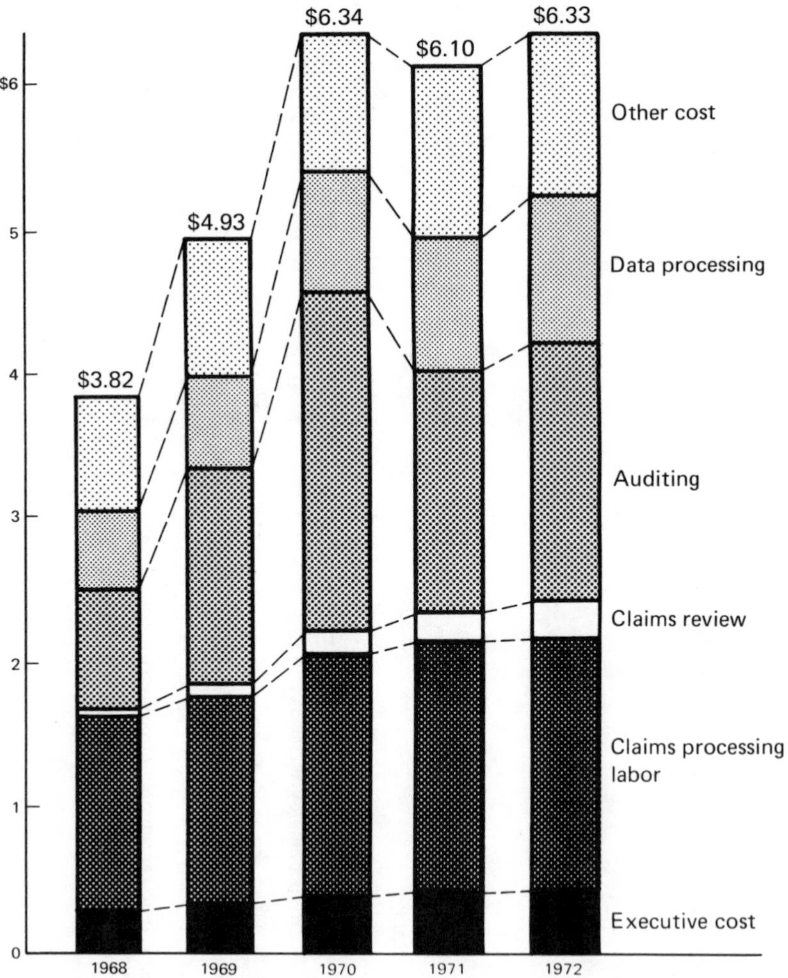

Figure 4-1. Components of Average Administrative Cost Per Bill, Part A, 1968-1972

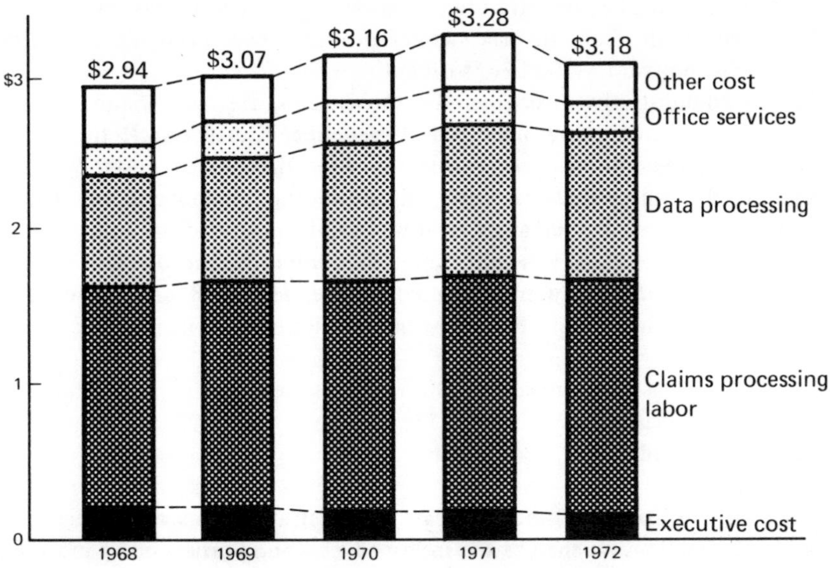

Figure 4-2. Components of Average Administrative Cost Per Claim, Medicare, Part B, 1968-1972

percentage of benefits paid or on a per enrollee basis, they are lower on a unit basis. This is not paradoxical precisely because Part A benefits were almost three times those of Part B benefits in 1972. Again, it is useful to remind the reader of the difficulties of making efficiency comparisons even within the Medicare program. If the "output" of Medicare were "number of claims paid," then Part B might appear to be more efficient. If Medicare "output" is "total benefits paid," i.e., payments to protect peoples' wealth position, or "payments per person enrolled," then Part A might be deemed administratively more efficient. About 30 percent of Part A administrative costs are devoted to provider audit and utilization review, and these are the costs that have increased the most rapidly over the five-year period. These functions are important because they contribute to the quality of the program and they help to keep total program costs down.[g] The ratio of administrative costs to benefit payments or premiums can distort operating results if the quality of the program process is not taken into account. Figure 4-1 is an example of how Medicare's ratio of administrative

[g]The optimal level of audits is that where the marginal cost of the audit equals the marginal saving in preventing an unallowable cost. This indicates that the optimal point of unallowable costs is not zero from an economist's point of view. In contrast, the politician may be forced to expend more on audits than is optimal.

costs to benefits paid could have been kept lower if there were less claims review and provider audit. Benefits paid would probably have been higher and the quality of the program would have suffered.

Part B administrative tasks, on the other hand, are more claims specific. Although labor costs have increased, large expenditures on electronic data processing equipment have been able to offset these labor costs. With the exception of data processing costs, most of the components of Part B administrative costs have remained relatively stable on a per claim basis. Because auditing and utilization review are more labor intensive and demand a higher skill mix than do the production-type activities under Part B, one would expect Part A administrative costs to be larger than Part B's on a per claim basis.

The Extent of Fiscal Agent Involvement in Medicare

Up to now, we have discussed Medicare administrative costs on an aggregated basis. In this section, we analyze the Intermediaries and Carriers on an individual firm basis. Tables 4-7, 4-8, and 4-9 indicate the extent to which fiscal agents are involved with Medicare. Blue Cross-Blue Shield data and data for the commercial insurers are released on a calendar year basis, while data for Medicare are issued for the fiscal year. In order to make the data compatible, Medicare data for fiscal 1971 and 1972 were averaged. Enrollment data for states where there are multiple Intermediaries, such as in New York or in Pennsylvania, are presented on a statewide basis. Strictly speaking, an Intermediary or Carrier does not have enrollees. The individual is enrolled under Medicare; he uses a hospital and the hospital is reimbursed by Blue Cross because the hospital has agreed to use Blue Cross as its Medicare Intermediary. If the individual chooses another hospital, that hospital may use another type of Intermediary such as a commercial insurer. As explained earlier, Carriers are assigned specific geographic areas.

The Blue Cross Intermediaries serve 74.9 million people under their regular business and 20.4 million people under Medicare. Their Medicare population amounts to 27 percent of their regular enrollees. For many of the Blue Cross Intermediaries, Medicare *benefits* as a percentage of regular business *benefits* (claims) are quite substantial; in a large proportion of cases they exceed 100 percent of regular business benefits. The Seattle, Jacksonville, and Great Falls plans, in particular, have the largest Medicare enrollment as a percentage of their regular business. There are basically three reasons for this phenomenon: First, the aged are twice as likely to be hospitalized as the rest of the population. Second, their average annual hospital bill is a little more than three times the average annual bill for the entire population.[7] Finally, Medicare benefit coverage is more extensive than that of many Blue Cross plans because Medicare covers extended care facilities and home health agencies.

While the mean Medicare administrative expense as a percentage of regular administrative expense is 18.4 percent, there is substantial variation around that mean. This is due to the fact that some Blue Cross Intermediaries are more efficient than others but especially due to the fact that some Blue Cross plans pay a larger percentage of Medicare benefits to regular benefits than others. Also, six Blue Cross and Blue Shield plans are merged. For example, in Alabama, Birmingham is the site of a merged Blue Cross-Blue Shield. Medicare Part A and Part B figures expressed as a percentage of Alabama's regular business will be a bit distorted in relation to figures for, say, Topeka, Kansas, where Blue Cross and Blue Shield are separate entities. Further, some Blue Cross plans have been more successful than others in selling coverage complementary to Medicare to the elderly. Complementary coverage is included in regular-business statistics.

The thirty-one Blue Shield plans which are Carriers under Medicare, Part B have an average Medicare enrollment coverage as a percentage of regular coverage of 22.5 percent. Medicare benefit payments as a percentage of regular benefit payments average 60.6 percent, but there is substantial variation among the plans. For example, the ratio for Jacksonville, Florida, is 368.4 percent while it is 20.1 percent in Birmingham, Alabama. The average Medicare administrative expense as a percentage of regular administrative expense is 45.6 percent. This ratio is higher than the comparable figure for the Blue Cross Intermediaries because regular Blue Shield business is less comparable to Part B than regular Blue Cross business to Part A. Regular Blue Shield does not have as many small bills as Medicare Part B because there is less outpatient coverage under regular Blue Shield business. Of the thirteen commercial Intermediaries and Carriers for which data are available, only three companies had Medicare benefits which exceeded 50 percent of regular benefits in 1971 and all three were relatively small health insurers. As with the Blue Cross-Blue Shield plans, administrative costs of Medicare as a percentage of regular administrative costs varied substantially.

Tables 4-10 and 4-11 provide comparisons of Medicare and regular business administrative expense and claims expense on a per enrollee basis as well as comparisons of administrative expense as a percentage of claims expense under both types of business for Blue Cross Intermediaries and Blue Shield Carriers. It was not possible to make similar comparisons for the commercial Intermediaries and Carriers because no data are available on their regular business customer enrollment. It would also have been interesting to make comparisons by Intermediary and by Carrier of average claim size, but the data for that comparison for Blue Cross-Blue Shield and commercial regular business remain confidential. As in Table 4-7, data for states where there are multiple Intermediaries are presented on an aggregated statewide basis. Examination of Table 4-10 reveals that, in general, administrative expenses on a per enrollee basis are higher under Blue Cross regular business than under Medicare Part A. There are, however, some exceptions: for example, Wilmington, Delaware, Blue Cross spent

Table 4-7
Blue Cross Plans: Number of Enrollees, Benefit Payments, and Administrative Costs Under Regular Business and Under Medicare, Calendar Year 1971

State and plan	Enrollees under–			Benefits paid under–			Administrative costs under–		
		Medicare			Medicare			Medicare	
	Regular business	Number	Percentage of regular business	Regular business	Amount	Percentage of regular business	Regular business	Amount	Percentage of regular business
Total	74,932,397	20,356,890	27.2	$6,053,538,788	$5,407,846,500	89.3	$338,909,565	$62,308,049	18.4
Alabama, Birmingham	1,162,628	338,827	29.1	[1] 120,569,959	73,869,500	61.3	6,051,164	516,810	8.5
Alaska[3]	–	–	–	–	–	–	–	–	–
Arizona, Phoenix	299,012	171,284	57.3	25,048,138	54,908,500	219.2	1,756,015	551,842	31.4
Arkansas, Little Rock	494,885	245,934	49.7	[1] 35,831,625	48,275,000	134.7	2,826,845	410,774	14.5
California	3,184,459	1,841,313	47.8	374,063,046	565,129,500	151.1	29,972,897	7,118,354	23.7
Los Angeles	1,676,184	–	–	[1] 205,773,940	347,463,500	168.9	15,377,238	4,102,018	26.7
Oakland	1,508,275	–	–	[1] 168,289,106	217,666,000	129.3	14,595,659	3,016,336	20.7
Colorado, Denver	890,179	194,668	21.9	68,986,293	65,079,500	94.3	4,348,021	869,504	20.0
Connecticut, New Haven	1,516,603	296,130	19.5	127,430,555	66,072,500	51.8	5,650,827	441,823	7.8
Delaware, Wilmington	402,349	46,664	11.6	30,674,677	12,711,000	41.4	1,091,816	200,368	18.4
District of Columbia, Washington[1]	1,374,225	151,442	4.8	93,744,917	39,877,500	42.5	5,179,981	418,790	8.1
Florida, Jacksonville	1,491,698	999,189	67.0	88,449,190	248,175,500	280.7	5,445,380	2,497,336	45.9
Georgia	946,578	379,811	40.1	56,420,592	71,371,500	126.5	3,256,912	1,140,542	35.0
Atlanta	468,456	–	–	32,721,115	29,085,500	88.9	1,683,306	522,958	31.1
Columbus	478,123	–	–	23,699,477	42,286,000	178.4	1,573,606	617,584	39.2
Hawaii[4]	–	–	–	–	–	–	–	–	–
Idaho, Boise	143,630	72,196	50.3	[1] 9,932,771	14,855,500	149.6	1,104,475	278,852	25.2

Illinois	3,089,616	1,110,171	35.9	306,700,264	349,486,500	114.0	17,536,605	3,505,936	20.0
Chicago	2,970,264	–	–	299,234,890	343,382,500	114.8	16,601,102	3,446,540	20.8
Rockford	119,352	–	–	[1] 7,465,374	6,104,000	81.8	935,503	59,395	6.3
Indiana, Indianapolis	1,888,277	505,070	26.7	148,333,927	122,943,500	82.9	12,480,910	1,832,332	14.7
Iowa	1,164,085	357,525	30.7	66,166,081	109,873,000	166.1	4,278,403	1,146,207	26.8
Des Moines	915,773	–	–	53,064,663	70,277,500	132.4	3,368,125	796,376	23.6
Sioux City	248,312	–	–	13,101,418	39,595,500	302.2	910,278	349,830	38.4
Kansas, Topeka	756,041	272,968	36.1	50,973,511	56,665,500	111.2	3,692,789	713,524	19.3
Kentucky, Louisville	1,206,118	347,044	28.8	66,662,441	72,329,000	108.5	3,329,759	1,034,523	31.1
Louisiana	866,310	314,475	36.3	63,085,408	75,346,500	119.4	5,599,477	1,045,894	18.7
Baton Rouge	550,087	–	–	[1] 34,546,483	47,643,000	137.9	3,394,213	633,020	18.6
New Orleans	316,223	–	–	[1] 28,538,925	27,703,500	97.1	2,205,264	412,873	18.7
Maine, Portland	431,926	123,148	28.5	27,027,376	28,368,000	105.0	1,585,783	409,754	25.8
Maryland, Baltimore	1,399,888	303,293	21.7	124,971,003	75,041,000	60.0	5,127,392	855,050	17.3
Massachusetts, Boston	3,139,769	640,048	20.4	305,842,000	208,481,000	68.2	11,920,000	2,755,761	23.1
Michigan, Detroit	5,071,300	784,439	15.5	469,146,000	255,309,500	54.4	20,539,000	3,030,734	14.8
Minnesota, St. Paul	892,557	421,246	47.2	67,354,396	126,729,000	188.2	5,120,086	1,579,236	30.8
Mississippi, Jackson	506,580	231,694	45.7	[1] 38,668,476	48,756,500	126.1	3,396,989	578,275	17.0
Missouri	1,797,954	569,461	31.7	146,787,263	169,070,000	115.2	7,334,508	2,128,978	29.0
Kansas City	539,173	–	–	44,439,818	56,847,000	127.9	2,631,212	463,057	17.6
St. Louis	1,258,781	–	–	102,347,445	112,223,000	109.6	4,703,296	1,665,922	35.4
Montana, Great Falls	81,749	71,350	87.3	[1] 7,195,823	17,812,500	247.5	777,142	220,758	28.7
Nebraska, Omaha	389,583	186,802	47.9	26,648,797	38,949,500	138.7	2,351,224	286,494	12.2
Nevada[1]	–	–	–	–	–	–	–	–	–
New Hampshire, Concord	565,634	133,303	15.0	33,944,451	33,477,000	98.6	1,967,935	604,361	30.7
New Jersey, Newark	3,695,572	711,571	19.3	274,760,000	129,917,500	47.3	11,727,257	1,240,200	10.6
New Mexico, Albuquerque	133,529	77,565	58.1	7,843,808	16,172,500	206.2	503,850	241,345	47.9

Table 4-7 (cont.)

State and plan	Enrollees under–			Benefits paid under–			Administrative costs under–		
		Medicare			Medicare			Medicare	
	Regular business	Number	Percentage of regular business	Regular business	Amount	Percentage of regular business	Regular business	Amount	Percentage of regular business
New York	11,811,175	1,981,767	16.8	799,998,412	642,106,000	80.3	46,944,371	6,394,612	13.6
Albany	544,828	–	–	42,948,633	40,484,000	94.3	2,390,121	392,887	16.4
Buffalo	978,536	–	–	65,277,806	48,781,500	74.7	3,819,522	626,660	16.4
Jamestown	61,720	–	–	2,632,809	5,163,000	196.1	127,915	74,325	58.1
New York City	8,526,423	–	–	581,126,826	456,102,000	78.5	35,707,304	4,414,959	12.4
Rochester	834,595	–	–	56,080,114	28,934,500	51.6	2,427,184	357,670	14.7
Syracuse	525,869	–	–	33,321,021	36,406,500	109.3	1,479,418	282,400	19.1
Utica	293,922	–	–	15,931,957	22,650,500	142.2	770,993	203,512	26.4
Watertown	45,282	–	–	2,679,252	3,579,500	133.6	221,911	42,199	19.0
North Carolina, Chapel Hill-Durham	1,552,106	435,456	28.1	[1] 125,513,000	93,462,500	74.5	8,308,000	1,102,854	13.1
North Dakota, Fargo	290,930	69,680	24.0	21,465,640	21,005,000	97.9	1,311,051	218,416	16.7
Ohio	5,420,810	1,014,633	18.7	454,581,245	271,628,000	59.8	17,099,555	2,933,280	17.2
Canton	236,239	–	–	17,698,567	11,195,000	63.3	587,270	138,180	23.5
Cincinnati	1,514,914	–	–	125,012,767	67,919,500	54.3	5,086,946	827,222	16.3
Cleveland	1,785,875	–	–	165,857,450	84,374,000	50.9	6,592,331	959,321	14.6
Columbus	735,439	–	–	46,999,923	45,069,000	95.9	1,646,776	477,713	29.8
Lima	145,306	–	–	8,268,247	8,320,500	100.6	273.222	70,849	25.9
Toledo	619,275	–	–	53,880,718	29,559,500	54.9	1,910,602	249,726	13.1
Youngstown	383,762	–	–	36,863,573	25,190,500	68.3	1,002,408	210,268	21.0
Oklahoma, Tulsa	619,647	305,178	49.2	44,176,293	72,114,500	163.2	2,412,014	924,704	38.3
Oregon, Portland	465,512	235,568	50.6	[1] 44,614,885	58,521,000	131.2	3,708,311	561,436	15.1
Pennsylvania	6,495,527	1,298,811	20.0	506,615,628	265,776,000	52.5	21,806,673	3,201,106	14.7
Allentown	389,907	–	–	23,733,790	11,723,000	49.4	1,177,869	135,930	11.5

Harrisburg	900,394	–	–	59,179,671	40,557,000	68.5	2,655,910	483,453	18.2
Philadelphia	2,391,466	–	–	203,623,706	56,280,500	27.6	6,985,061	623,696	8.9
Pittsburgh	2,293,211	–	–	185,538,738	127,880,500	68.9	9,754,081	1,627,562	16.7
Wilkes-Barre	520,549	–	–	34,539,723	29,735,000	86.1	1,233,752	330,466	26.8
Rhode Island, Providence	714,630	106,679	14.9	53,726,867	34,464,500	64.1	2,084,063	443,403	21.3
South Carolina, Columbia	488,885	202,550	41.4	30,875,256	36,454,500	118.1	2,042,685	758,294	37.1
South Dakota[5]	–	–	–	–	–	–	–	–	–
Tennessee	1,351,871	399,601	29.6	109,064,847	94,813,500	86.9	8,094,697	1,125,576	13.9
Chattanooga	1,161,860	–	–	[1] 89,679,319	72,060,000	80.4	6,295,037	816,826	13.0
Memphis	190,011	–	–	[1] 19,385,528	22,753,500	117.4	1,709,660	308,750	17.2
Texas, Dallas	2,802,691	1,026,809	36.6	[1] 292,632,278	275,047,500	94.0	18,304,225	2,615,731	14.3
Utah, Salt Lake City	319,423	81,032	25.4	19,550,507	16,414,500	84.0	1,249,898	304,055	24.3
Vermont[6]	–	–	–	–	–	–	–	–	–
Virginia	1,174,333	378,494	32.2	81,559,536	72,820,500	89.3	4,390,170	990,940	22.6
Richmond	869,226	–	–	61,007,145	58,109,000	95.2	3,698,193	831,459	22.5
Roanoke	305,107	–	–	20,552,391	14,711,500	71.6	691,977	159,482	23.0
Washington, Seattle	444,872	333,472	75.0	[1] 40,023,340	64,691,500	161.6	4,398,203	718,759	16.3
West Virginia	387,012	202,777	52.4	30,884,741	45,045,500	145.8	1,207,641	660,696	54.7
Bluefield	30,014	–	–	194,051	–	–	104,024	–	–
Charleston	204,690	–	–	15,493,851	23,517,500	151.8	675,922	287,038	42.5
Parkersburg	40,352	–	–	3,466.814	5,342,500	154.1	107,468	73,978	68.5
Wheeling	111,956	–	–	9,975,025	16,185,500	162.3	320,227	299,680	93.6
Wisconsin, Milwaukee	1,509,551	487,725	32.3	130,532,111	132,298,500	101.4	9,197,055	1,340,414	14.6
Wyoming, Cheyenne	100,688	31,876	31.7	4,461,429	6,871,000	154.0	307,511	104,854	34.1

Source: Unpublished Social Security Administration data and *Blue Cross-Blue Shield Fact Book, 1972.*

Notes: 1. Includes surgical-medical plan.
2. Served by Seattle, Washington plan.
3. Includes enrollees in covered Maryland and Virginia counties.
4. No Blue Cross plan.
5. Served by Iowa plan.
6. Served by New Hampshire plan.

Table 4-8
Blue Shield Plans: Number of Enrollees, Benefit Payments, and Administrative Costs Under Regular Business and Under Medicare, Calendar Year 1971

[In thousands, except for percentages]

State and plan	Enrollees under–			Benefit payments under–			Administrative costs under–		
		Medicare			Medicare			Medicare	
	Regular business	Number	Percent of regular business	Regular business	Amount	Percent of regular business	Regular business	Amount	Percent of regular business
Total	48,745	10,974	22.5	$1,860,747	$1,127,292	60.6	$233,910	$102,125	45.6
Alabama, Birmingham	1,136	315	27.7	[1] 120,570	24,241	20.1	6,051	1,800	29.7
Arkansas, Little Rock	484	225	46.5	[1] 35,832	15,355	42.9	2,827	1,477	52.3
California, San Francisco	1,139	724	63.6	[1] 114,290	134,738	117.9	21,682	15,752	72.6
Colorado, Denver	847	177	20.9	27,585	19,193	69.6	3,967	2,588	65.2
Delaware, Wilmington	375	42	11.2	11,744	3,062	26.1	1,216	375	30.8
District of Columbia, Washington[2]	1,312	146	4.6	83,574	18,206	21.8	9,707	1,879	19.4
Florida, Jacksonville	1,444	936	64.8	34,031	125,360	368.4	5,598	7,423	132.6
Illinois	2,649	469	17.7	64,043	49,584	77.4	9,415	5,071	53.9
Indiana, Indianapolis	1,846	459	24.9	67,011	31,762	47.4	6,273	2,723	43.4
Iowa, Des Moines	1,030	333	32.3	47,036	19,586	41.6	5,330	2,376	44.6
Kansas, Topeka	756	244	32.3	30,970	15,555	50.2	3,677	1,829	49.7
Maryland, Baltimore	1,283	272	21.2	41,387	14,870	35.9	4,504	1,654	36.7
Massachusetts, Boston	3,035	610	20.1	103,658	62,579	60.4	13,036	5,546	42.5
Michigan, Detroit	4,888	737	15.1	280,409	65,126	23.2	24,668	7,389	30.0
Minnesota, Minneapolis	609	214	35.1	34,774	10,440	30.0	6,773	1,267	18.7
Missouri	1,491	146	9.8	49,075	14,517	29.6	7,274	1,430	19.7

Montana, Helena	109	63	57.6	[1] 9,080	4,460	49.1	1,008	294	29.2
New Hampshire, Concord	551	125	22.7	16,907	9,154	54.1	2,591	995	38.4
New York	9,314	1,298	13.9	218,869	178,429	81.5	32,322	16,461	50.9
North Dakota, Fargo	287	64	22.4	10,933	4,903	44.8	1,663	541	32.5
Pennsylvania, Camp Hill	5,931	1,176	19.8	157,122	102,202	65.0	19,535	7,026	36.0
Rhode Island, Providence	701	102	14.6	20,179	10,269	50.9	2,074	779	37.5
South Carolina, Columbia	473	186	39.3	9,335	10,045	107.6	2,069	1,043	50.4
South Dakota, Sioux Falls	95	78	82.1	1,682	4,291	255.1	409	464	113.6
Texas, Dallas	2,806	955	34.1	36,290	103,936	286.4	5,894	6,934	117.7
Utah, Salt Lake City	317	70	22.2	14,508	5,469	37.7	1,640	431	26.3
Virginia	1,139	28	2.5	36,704	–	–	3,918	–	–
Washington	696	309	44.4	[1] 73,802	28,054	38.0	7,320	3,290	44.9
Wisconsin	1,780	458	25.7	[1] 91,677	34,290	37.4	9,751	2,627	26.9
Puerto Rico	222	98	44.4	17,670	7.616	43.1	1,723	661	38.4

Source: Unpublished data of the Social Security Administration and *Blue Cross-Blue Shield Fact Book, 1972.*

Notes: 1. Includes hospital plan.

2. Includes enrollees in covered Maryland and Virginia counties.

Table 4-9

Commercial Insurance Companies: Claims Payments, Benefit Payments, and Administrative Costs Under Regular Business and Under Medicare, Calendar Year 1971

Insurance company	Claims payment under regular business	Benefit payments under Medicare: Total: Amount	Benefit payments under Medicare: Total: Percentage of regular business	Benefit payments under Medicare: Hospital insurance	Benefit payments under Medicare: Supplementary medical insurance	Administrative costs under regular business	Administrative costs under Medicare: Total: Amount	Administrative costs under Medicare: Total: Percentage of regular business	Administrative costs under Medicare: Hospital insurance	Administrative costs under Medicare: Supplementary medical insurance
Total	$5,311,854	$1,045,272	19.7	$411,019	$634,552	$868,791	$61,289	7.1	$8,482	$52,807
Aetna	977,336	211,547	21.6	151,758	59,789	115,709	8,003	6.9	2,636	5,367
Connecticut General	515,444	24,940	4.8	–	24,940	66,983	1,628	2.4	–	1,628
Continental Casualty	43,868	29,220	66.6	–	29,220	15,783	3,130	19.8	–	3,130
Equitable	560,471	37,612	6.7	–	37,612	77,528	3,380	4.4	–	3,380
General American	82,335	28,428	34.5	–	28,428	11,922	2,362	19.8	–	2,362
Metropolitan	768,584	43,114	5.6	–	43,114	138,449	5,406	3.9	–	5,406
Mutual of Omaha	354,288	65,418	18.5	52,511	12,907	129,945	2,946	2.3	1,784	1,162
Nationwide	31,076	87,525	281.6	21,940	65,584	8,234	6,222	75.6	342	5,880
Occidental	239,401	112,858	47.1	–	112,858	27,453	8,453	30.8	–	8,453
Pan American	21,908	20,250	92.4	–	20,250	5,602	1,773	31.6	–	1,773
Prudential	720,032	191,434	26.4	63,908	127,526	141,117	10,600	7.5	956	9,644
Travelers	889,346	186,460	21.0	120,902	65,558	109,879	6.612	6.0	2,764	3,848
Union Mutual	101,745	6,766	6.6	–	6,766	20,187	774	3.8	–	774

Source: Unpublished Social Security Administration data and *1972 Argus Chart of Health Insurance.*

$4.29 per Medicare enrollee in 1971 and $2.71 per regular business enrollee, and New Hampshire Blue Cross spent $4.53 per Medicare enrollee and $3.48 per regular business enrollee. This pattern is not typical, however; in only seven instances were Medicare administrative expenses higher than regular business expenses on a per enrollee basis. In contrast, Medicare benefit payments per enrollee are consistently higher than regular business claims expense. For the United States total, Medicare benefit payments on a per enrollee basis are over three times that of regular business claims payments on a per enrollee basis. Because the average benefit payment under Medicare is much higher than under regular business and because average regular business administrative expense is not much greater than average Medicare administrative expense, administrative expense as a percentage of Medicare benefits is consistently much lower than regular business administrative expense as a percentage of claims expense.

Table 4-11 reveals a somewhat different pattern for the Carriers. In general, administrative expenses per enrollee under Medicare are higher than under regular business. Although benefit payments per enrollee are higher under Medicare than under regular business, the difference is not as large as for the Intermediaries. As a consequence, the ratio of administrative expenses to benefits paid under Medicare is not dissimilar to the same ratio under regular business.

Table 4-12 ranks the Intermediaries using three different measures of administrative efficiency. When one searches for reasons why some Intermediaries rank below the national average on the three measures, one sees that the commercial Intermediaries fall below the average with greater frequency than the Blue Cross Intermediaries. This is not coincidental, but is not a measure of true relative efficiency. The commercial Intermediaries deal relatively more extensively with extended care facilities (ECF) than do the Blue Cross Intermediaries. Because the American Hospital Association nominated Blue Cross as Intermediary under Medicare and because most hospitals are members of the AHA and supported the nomination, Blue Cross became an Intermediary for most hospitals. The commercial companies were nominated as Intermediaries for some hospitals and many ECFs.

When one observes Figure 4-3 showing the relationship between unit costs and the percentage of bills that come from the ECF, one notes that as that percentage moves upward, unit costs increase commensurately. One of the reasons why administrative costs are higher for those firms dealing more extensively with the ECF is that the claims review effort is greater for ECFs than in the case for hospitals. Often, for ECF claims, a determination must be made whether care given to the elderly by the ECF is merely custodial or care covered by the Medicare law. Medicare does not reimburse for the former. This determination of level and type of care has proved to be administratively expensive. Another reason why ECF bills have been costly to process is the high percentage of bill errors, which may be due to the frequent changes in ECF ownership and to greatest staff turnover.

Table 4-10
Blue Cross Intermediaries: Benefit Payments and Administrative Costs Per Enrollee and Administrative Costs as Percentage of Benefit Payments Under Regular Business and Under Medicare, Calendar Year 1971

State and plan	Benefit payments per enrollee		Administrative costs per enrollee		Administrative costs as percent of benefit payments	
	Regular business	Medicare	Regular business	Medicare	Regular business	Medicare
Total	$80.79	$265.65	$4.52	$3.06	5.6	1.2
	[2] 103.70	218.02	5.20	1.53	5.0	7
Alaska[1]	–	–	–	–	–	–
Arizona, Phoenix	83.77	29.02	5.87	3.22	7.0	1.0
Arkansas, Little Rock	[2] 72.41	196.29	5.71	1.67	7.9	.8
California	117.47	306.92	9.41	3.87	8.0	1.3
Los Angeles	[1] 109.74	–	8.20	–	7.5	1.2
Oakland	[2] 111.58	–	9.68	–	8.7	1.4
Colorado, Denver	77.50	334.39	4.88	4.47	6.3	1.3
Connecticut, New Haven	84.02	223.12	3.73	1.49	4.4	.7
Delaware, Wilmington	76.24	272.39	2.71	4.29	3.6	.8
District of Columbia, Washington[3]	68.22	263.32	3.77	2.77	5.5	1.0
Florida, Jacksonville	59.30	248.49	3.65	2.50	6.2	1.0
Georgia	59.60	187.91	3.44	3.00	5.8	1.6
Atlanta	70.30	–	3.62	–	5.1	1.8
Columbus	49.57	–	3.29	–	6.6	1.5
Hawaii[4]	–	–	–	–	–	–
Idaho, Boise	[2] 69.16	205.77	7.69	3.86	11.1	1.9

Illinois	99.27	314.80	5.68	3.16	5.7	1.0
Chicago	100.74	–	5.59	–	5.5	1.0
Rockford	[2] 62.55	–	7.84	–	12.5	1.0
Indiana, Indianapolis	78.56	243.42	6.61	3.63	8.4	1.5
Iowa	56.86	185.06	3.67	3.21	6.5	1.0
Des Moines	57.95	–	3.68	–	6.3	1.1
Sioux City	53.85	–	3.74	–	6.9	.9
Kansas, Topeka	67.42	207.59	4.88	2.61	7.2	1.3
Kentucky, Louisville	55.27	208.41	2.76	2.98	5.0	1.4
Louisiana	72.82	239.60	6.46	3.33	8.9	1.4
Baton Rouge	[2] 62.81	–	6.17	–	9.8	1.3
New Orleans	[2] 90.25	–	6.97	–	7.7	1.5
Maine, Portland	62.57	230.36	3.67	3.33	5.9	1.4
Maryland, Baltimore	89.28	247.42	3.66	2.82	4.1	1.1
Massachusetts, Boston	97.41	325.73	3.80	4.31	3.9	1.3
Michigan, Detroit	92.51	347.63	4.05	4.13	4.4	1.2
Minnesota, St. Paul	75.46	300.84	5.74	3.75	7.6	1.2
Mississippi, Jackson	[2] 76.33	210.43	6.71	2.50	8.8	1.2
Missouri	81.62	296.89	4.08	3.73	5.0	1.3
Kansas City	82.42	–	4.88	–	5.9	.8
St. Louis	81.31	–	3.74	–	4.6	1.5
Montana, Great Falls	[2] 88.02	249.65	9.51	2.81	10.8	1.2
Nebraska, Omaha	68.40	197.80	6.04	1.53	8.8	.8
Nevada[4]	–	–	–	–	–	–
New Hampshire, Concord	60.11	251.13	3.48	4.53	5.8	1.8
New Jersey, Newark	74.35	182.58	3.17	1.74	4.3	1.0
New Mexico, Albuquerque	58.74	208.50	3.77	3.11	6.4	1.5
New York	67.73	824.01	3.97	3.23	5.9	1.0

Table 4-10 (cont.)

State and plan	Benefit payments per enrollee		Administrative costs per enrollee		Administrative costs as percent of benefit payments	
	Regular business	Medicare	Regular business	Medicare	Regular business	Medicare
Albany	78.83	–	4.31	–	5.5	1.0
Buffalo	66.71	–	3.90	–	5.9	1.3
Jamestown	42.66	–	2.07	–	4.9	1.4
New York City	68.16	–	4.19	–	6.1	1.0
Rochester	67.19	–	2.91	–	4.3	1.2
Syracuse	63.36	–	2.81	–	4.4	.8
Utica	52.84	–	2.62	–	5.0	.9
Watertown	59.17	–	4.90	–	8.3	1.2
North Carolina, Chapel Hill-Durham	[2] 80.87	214.63	5.41	2.53	6.7	1.2
North Dakota, Fargo	73.78	301.67	4.51	3.14	6.1	1.0
Ohio	83.86	267.71	3.15	2.89	3.8	1.1
Canton	74.92	–	2.49	–	3.3	1.2
Cincinnati	82.52	–	3.34	–	4.1	1.2
Cleveland	93.92	–	3.73	–	4.0	1.1
Columbus	63.91	–	2.24	–	3.5	1.1
Lima	56.90	–	1.88	–	3.3	9
Toledo	87.01	–	3.09	–	3.5	8
Youngstown	96.03	–	2.61	–	2.7	.8
Oklahoma, Tulsa	71.29	236.30	3.89	3.03	5.5	1.3
Oregon, Portland	[2] 95.84	248.43	7.97	2.34	8.3	.9
Pennsylvania	77.99	205.10	3.36	2.47	4.3	1.2
Allentown	60.87	–	3.02	–	5.0	1.2

Harrisburg	65.73	–	2.95	–	4.5	1.2
Philadelphia	85.15	–	2.92	–	3.4	1.1
Pittsburgh	80.91	–	4.25	–	5.3	1.3
Wilkes-Barre	66.35	–	2.37	–	3.6	1.1
Rhode Island, Providence	75.18	323.07	2.87	4.16	3.8	1.3
South Carolina, Columbia	63.81	179.98	4.22	3.74	6.6	2.1
South Dakota[5]	–	–	–	–	–	–
Tennessee	80.68	237.27	5.99	2.82	7.4	1.2
Chattanooga	[2] 77.19	–	5.42	–	7.0	1.1
Memphis	[2] 102.02	–	9.47	–	9.3	1.4
Texas, Dallas	[2] 104.41	267.87	6.53	2.55	6.3	1.0
Utah, Salt Lake City	61.21	202.57	3.91	3.75	6.4	1.9
Vermont[6]	–	–	–	–	–	–
Virginia	69.45	192.40	3.74	2.62	5.4	1.4
Richmond	70.22	–	4.25	–	6.1	1.4
Roanoke	67.36	–	2.27	–	3.4	1.1
Washington, Seattle	[2] 89.97	193.99	10.50	2.16	11.0	1.1
West Virginia	79.80	222.14	3.12	3.26	3.9	1.5
Bluefield	15.38	–	10.39	–	5.3	–
Charleston	75.69	–	3.30	–	4.4	1.0
Parkersburg	85.90	–	2.66	–	3.1	1.4
Wheeling	89.10	–	2.77	–	3.1	1.9
Wisconsin, Milwaukee	86.47	302.23	6.09	3.06	7.0	1.0
Wyoming, Cheyenne	44.31	215.55	3.35	3.29	7.6	1.6

Source: Unpublished Social Security Administration data and *Blue Cross-Blue Shield Fact Book, 1972.*

Notes:
1. Served by Seattle, Washington plan.
2. Includes surgical-medical plan.
3. Includes enrollees in covered Maryland and Virginia counties.
4. No Blue Cross plan.
5. Served by Iowa plan.
6. Served by New Hampshire plan.

Table 4-11
Blue Shield Carriers: Benefit Payments and Administrative Costs Per Enrollee and Administrative Costs as Percentage of Benefit Payments Under Regular Business and Under Medicare, Calendar Year 1971

State and plan	Benefit payments per enrollee		Administrative costs per enrollee		Administrative costs as percent of benefit payments	
	Regular business	Medicare	Regular business	Medicare	Regular business	Medicare
Total	$38.17	$102.72	$4.80	$9.31	12.6	9.1
Alabama, Birmingham	[1] 106.14	76.96	5.33	5.71	5.0	7.4
Arkansas, Little Rock	[1] 74.03	68.24	5.84	6.56	7.9	9.6
California, San Francisco	[1] 100.34	186.10	19.04	21.76	19.0	11.7
Colorado, Denver	32.57	108.44	4.68	14.62	14.4	13.5
Delaware, Wilmington	31.32	72.90	3.24	8.93	10.4	12.2
District of Columbia, Washington[2]	63.70	124.70	7.40	12.07	11.6	10.3
Florida, Jacksonville	23.57	133.93	3.88	7.93	16.4	5.9
Illinois	24.18	105.72	3.55	10.81	14.7	10.2
Indiana, Indianapolis	36.30	69.20	3.40	5.93	9.4	8.6
Iowa, Des Moines	45.67	58.82	5.17	7.14	11.3	12.1
Kansas, Topeka	40.97	63.75	4.86	7.50	11.9	11.8
Maryland, Baltimore	32.26	54.67	3.51	6.08	10.9	11.1
Massachusetts, Boston	34.15	102.59	4.30	9.09	12.6	8.9
Michigan, Detroit	57.37	88.37	5.05	10.03	8.8	11.3
Minnesota, Minneapolis	57.10	48.79	11.12	5.92	19.5	12.1
Missouri	32.91	99.43	4.88	9.79	14.8	9.8
Montana, Helena	[1] 83.30	70.79	9.25	4.67	11.1	6.6
New Hampshire, Concord	30.68	73.23	4.70	7.96	15.3	10.9

New York	23.50	137.46	3.47	12.68	14.8	9.2
North Dakota, Fargo	38.09	76.61	5.79	8.45	15.2	11.0
Pennsylvania, Camp Hill	26.49	86.91	3.29	5.97	12.4	6.9
Rhode Island, Providence	28.79	100.68	2.96	7.64	10.3	7.6
South Carolina, Columbia	9.59	54.01	2.13	5.61	22.2	10.4
South Dakota, Sioux Falls	17.71	55.01	4.31	5.95	24.3	10.8
Texas, Dallas	12.93	108.83	2.10	7.26	16.2	6.7
Utah, Salt Lake City	45.77	78.13	5.17	6.16	11.3	7.9
Virginia	32.22	–	3.44	–	10.7	–
Washington	106.04	90.79	10.52	10.65	9.9	11.7
Wisconsin	[1] 51.50	74.87	5.48	5.74	10.6	7.7
Puerto Rico	79.59	77.71	7.76	6.74	9.8	8.7

Source: Unpublished Social Security Administration data and *Blue Cross-Blue Shield Fact Book, 1972.*

Notes: 1. Includes hospital plan.
2. Includes enrollees in covered Maryland and Virginia counties.

Table 4-12
Selected Data for HI Intermediaries Excluding Audit, Fiscal Year 1972

Administrative expenses as percentage of benefit payments		Unit cost[1]		Production per man-year bills	
National average[2]	1.25	National average[2]	$4.52	National average[2]	2,857
Kaiser	.30	Inter-County	2.41	Inter-County	4,493
Birmingham, Ala.	.76	Birmingham, Ala.	2.55	Utica, N.Y.	4,318
New Haven, Conn.	.79	Utica, N.Y.	2.63	Little Rock, Ark.	4,314
Omaha, Neb.	.80	Lima, Ohio	2.79	Birmingham, Ala.	4,231
Syracuse, N.Y.	.81	Charleston, W.Va.	2.83	New Haven, Conn.	4,092
Inter-County	.81	Syracuse, N.Y.	2.84	Lima, Ohio	4,023
Kansas City, Mo.	.84	Omaha, Neb.	2.99	Sioux City, Iowa	3,972
Chicago, Ill.	.92	Little Rock, Ark.	3.11	Charleston, W.Va.	3,945
Lima, Ohio	.93	Harrisburg, Pa.	3.20	Omaha, Neb.	3,932
Youngstown, Ohio	.94	New Haven, Conn.	3.31	Baltimore, Md.	3,894
Utica, N.Y.	.95	Roanoke, Va.	3.33	Rochester, N.Y.	3,822
Sioux City, Iowa	.96	Kansas City, Mo.	3.34	Syracuse, N.Y.	3,798
Dallas, Texas	.98	Watertown, N.Y.	3.36	Portland, Oreg.	3,752
Little Rock, Ark.	1.00	Wilkes-Barre, Pa.	3.36	Albany, N.Y.	3,751
New York, N.Y.	1.00	Jackson, Miss.	3.38	Philadelphia, Pa.	3,709
Toledo, Ohio	1.00	Pittsburgh, Pa.	3.42	Dallas, Texas	3,683
Portland, Oreg.	1.02	Sioux City, Iowa	3.43	Toledo, Ohio	3,640
Jacksonville, Fla.	1.02	Parkersburg, W.Va.	3.44	Boise, Idaho	3,626
Albany, N.Y.	1.03	Allentown, Pa.	3.48	Youngstown, Ohio	3,608
Newark, N.J.	1.06	Youngstown, Ohio	3.48	Harrisburg, Pa.	3,588
Columbus, Ohio	1.07	Chattanooga, Tenn.	3.53	Chapel Hill, N.C.	3,561
Milwaukee, Wis.	1.07	Albany, N.Y.	3.57	Providence, R.I.	3,553
Phoenix, Ariz.	1.07	Columbus, Ga.	3.63	Kaiser	3,528
Chattanooga, Tenn.	1.08	Toledo, Ohio	3.66	Pittsburgh, Pa.	3,512
Philadelphia, Pa.	1.08	Baltimore, Md.	3.67	Parkersburg, W.Va.	3,479
Jackson, Miss.	1.12	Kaiser	3.68	Chicago, Ill.	3,474
Washington, D.C.	1.12	Portland, Oreg.	3.68	Columbus, Ga.	3,464
Roanoke, Va.	1.14	Chapel Hill, N.C.	3.71	Chattanooga, Tenn.	3,389
Rockford, Ill.	1.14	Rockford, Ill.	3.72	Jackson, Miss.	3,381
Fargo, N. Dak.	1.15	Portland, Maine	3.76	Seattle, Wash.	3,380
Watertown, N.Y.	1.15	Columbus, Ohio	3.85	Rockford, Ill.	3,328
Cleveland, Ohio	1.17	Cooperativa	3.86	Baton Rouge, La.	3,290
Allentown, Pa.	1.19	Louisville, Ky.	3.93	Washington, D.C.	2,197
Des Moines, Iowa	1.19	Baton Rouge, La.	3.98	Allentown, Pa.	3,195
Baltimore, Md.	1.19	Philadelphia, Pa.	3.98	Milwaukee, Wis.	3,195
Harrisburg, Pa.	1.20	Jacksonville, Fla.	3.99	St. Paul, Minn.	3,195

Table 4-12 (cont.)

Administrative expenses as percentage of benefit payments		Unit cost[1]		Production per man-year bills	
Seattle, Wash.	1.20	Milwaukee, Wis.	4.00	San Juan, P.R.	3,193
Canton, Ohio	1.22	Rochester, N.Y.	4.01	Columbus, Ohio	3,141
Denver, Colo.	1.23	Dallas, Texas	4.02	Atlanta, Ga.	3,134
St. Paul, Minn.	1.24	Hawaii Medical	4.03	Roanoke, Va.	3,134
Wilkes-Barre, Pa.	1.24	Des Moines, Iowa	4.05	Louisville, Ky.	3,092
Chapel Hill, N.C.	1.25	Canton, Ohio	4.07	Canton, Ohio	3,092
Los Angeles, Calif.	1.25	Providence, R.I.	4.09	Wilmington, Del.	3,076
Rochester, N.Y.	1.26	Chicago, Ill.	4.11	Richmond, Va.	3,057
Providence, R.I.	1.27	Boise, Idaho	4.13	Wilkes-Barre, Pa.	3,050
Charleston, W.Va.	1.29	Seattle, Wash.	4.23	Cleveland, Ohio	2,994
Hawaii Medical	1.29	Buffalo, N.Y.	4.30	Boston, Mass.	2,993
Pittsburgh, Pa.	1.29	Phoenix, Ariz.	4.36	Phoenix, Ariz.	2,993
Richmond, Va.	1.29	Great Falls, Mont.	4.38	Jacksonville, Fla.	2,988
Parkersburg, W.Va.	1.30	San Juan, P.R.	4.41	Des Moines, Iowa	2,975
Boston, Mass.	1.32	Topeka, Kan.	4.47	Kansas City, Mo.	2,969
Buffalo, N.Y.	1.32	Fargo, N.D.	4.47	Watertown, N.Y.	2,896
Cincinnati, Ohio	1.33	Richmond, Va.	4.48	Newark, N.J.	2,873
Detroit, Mich	1.35	Wilmington, Del	4.50	Buffalo, N.Y.	2,866
Topeka, Kans.	1.35	St. Louis, Mo.	4.56	Portland, Maine	2,802
Great Falls, Mont.	1.36	Denver, Colo.	4.59	Cheyenne, Wyo.	2,780
Tulsa, Okla.	1.38	Newark, N.J.	4.60	Wheeling, W.Va.	2,727
Memphis, Tenn.	1.40	Prudential	4.61	Cincinnati, Ohio	2,713
Jamestown, N.Y.	1.42	Cleveland, Ohio	4.63	St. Louis, Mo.	2,688
Baton Rouge, La.	1.43	St. Paul, Minn.	4.63	Great Falls, Mont.	2,676
Louisville, Ky	1.46	Cheyenne, Wyo.	4.64	Topeka, Kan.	2,663
Prudential	1.50	Jamestown, N.Y.	4.73	Detroit, Mich.	2,649
St. Louis, Mo.	1.50	New Orleans, La.	4.73	Fargo, N. Dak.	2,646
Albuquerque, N. Mex.	1.52	Memphis, Tenn.	4.76	Oakland, Calif.	2,644
Oakland, Calif.	1.52	Atlanta, Ga.	4.77	Indianapolis, Ind.	2,599
Cooperativa	1.53	Nationwide	4.80	Memphis, Tenn.	2,583
Columbus, Ga.	1.54	Concord, N.H.	4.81	Albuquerque, N. Mex.	2,533
Portland, Maine	1.54	Boston, Mass.	4.87	Denver, Colo.	2,478
New Orleans, La.	1.58	Washington, D.C.	4.87	Jamestown, N.Y.	2,468
Indianapolis, Ind.	1.59	Albuquerque, N. Mex.	4.90	Prudential	2,434
Cheyenne, Wyo.	1.61	Wheeling, W.Va.	4.91	Cooperativa	2,404
Nationwide	1.70	Detroit, Mich.	5.03	Hawaii Medical	2,400
Wilmington, Del.	1.72	Cincinnati, Ohio	5.04	Nationwide	2,399
Aetna	1.72	Columbia, S.C.	5.12	Los Angeles, Calif.	2,357

Table 4-12 (cont.)

Administrative expenses as percentage of benefit payments		Unit cost[1]		Production per man-year bills	
Atlanta, Ga.	1.85	Indianapolis, Ind.	5.23	Concord, N.H.	2,335
Boise, Idaho	1.85	Oakland, Calif.	5.32	Salt Lake City, Utah	2,263
Wheeling, W.Va.	1.92	Tulsa, Okla.	5.55	Tulsa, Okla.	2,211
Concord, N.H.	1.97	Salt Lake City, Utah	5.68	New Orleans, La.	2,174
Salt Lake City, Utah	2.15	Los Angeles, Calif.	5.74	New York, N.Y.	2,154
Columbia, S.C.	2.18	New York, N.Y.	5.92	Aetna	2,105
Travelers	2.31	Aetna[3]	7.06	Columbia, S.C.	2,082
San Juan, P.R.	2.60	Travelers	8.85	Mutual of Omaha	1,340
Mutual of Omaha	3.63	Mutual of Omaha	9.21	Travelers	1,310

Source: Unpublished Social Security Administration data.

Notes:

1. All Blue Cross plan indices adjusted for Blue Cross Association overhead factors.

2. Weighted national average.

3.,Administrative costs include nonrecurring costs related to developing electronic data-processing systems for SSA. The adjusted figures are: administrative costs (excluding audit) $2,226,490, unit cost per bill, $5.61, and work load related cost $5.11.

Table 4-13 contains a similar ranking for Medicare Carriers. Unit cost and production per man year are presented on both a payment record and per claim basis. According to the Bureau of Health Insurance, the primary reason why firms fall below the national average in at least two of the three measures of efficiency presented has to do with changes in electronic data processing systems during the period considered.[h] As has been previously discussed, data processing is an important component of the Part B Carrier's administrative costs. To the extent that some Carriers have not yet adequately adopted an efficient EDP system or are not using it to its full capacity, their administrative costs will be high relative to those of other Carriers.

Theory of Fiduciary Involvement in Medicare Administration

In Chapter 3, we considered the theory of the nonprofit firm in order to gain some insight into the shape of Blue Cross-Blue Shield cost functions. Here, we extend that theory for purposes of understanding fiduciary involvement in the administration of Medicare. As explained earlier in this chapter, the Intermediaries under Medicare Part A and the Carriers under Medicare Part B are

[h]The Bureau of Health Insurance monitors Carrier data processing systems and maintains an annual narrative account of Carrier electronic of Carrier electronic data processing progress.

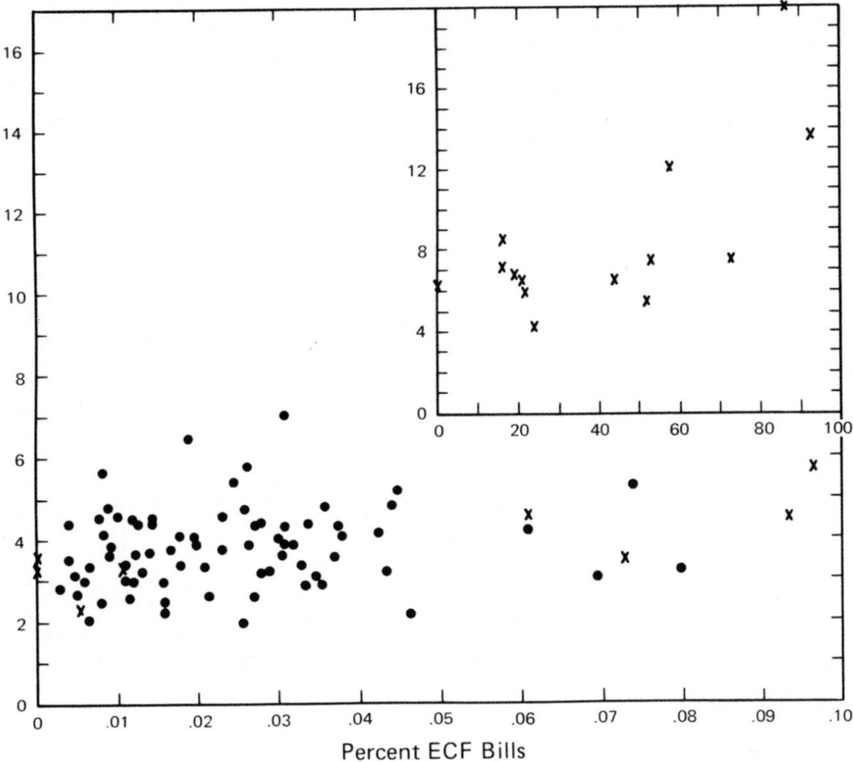

Figure 4-3. Intermediary Cost Per Claim and Percentage of Claims from Extended Care Facilities, Fiscal 1971

reimbursed for their administrative duties at cost. If the reimbursement mechanism is tightly controlled, the Intermediaries and Carriers cannot allocate any of their own-business costs to Medicare costs. This seems, at first blush, to preclude their gaining any advantage by acquiring Intermediary or Carrier status. But Tables 4-7, 4-8, and 4-9 reveal that these fiscal agents are deeply involved with Medicare. Thus, the government has experienced little difficulty in finding firms to handle a significant increase in their administrative workload. This clearly makes economic sense if these fiscal agents experience economies of scale in the administration of health insurance.

Consider Figure 4-4, which depicts the average (AC) and marginal costs (MC) of administering health insurance in the presence of economies of scale. Suppose that the number of claims for the firm's own business is given by *OI* and the average cost of administering this volume of claims is *OA*. The total cost of

Table 4-13
Selected Data for SMI Carriers, Fiscal Year 1972

Administrative expenses as percentage of benefit payments		Unit cost			Production per man-year bills		
			Payment record	Claim		Payment record	Claim
National Average[1]	8.77	National Average[1]	$3.93	$3.18	National Average[1]	2,905	3,590
Jacksonville, Fla.	5.83	Providence, R.I.	2.23	1.57	Providence, R.I.	5,339	7,591
Madison, Wis.	6.38	Madison, Wis.	2.85	2.07	Dallas, Tex.	4,129[3]	5,331
Connecticut General	6.52	San Juan, P.R.	3.00	2.86	Madison, Wis.	4,065	5,582
Camp Hill, Pa.	6.77	Connecticut General	3.03	2.68	Rochester, N.Y.	3,997	4,628
Dallas, Tex.	6.89	Camp Hill, Pa.	3.07	2.77	Camp Hill, Pa.	3,909[1]	4,332
Prudential	7.16	Jacksonville, Fla.	3.09	3.01	Boston, Mass.	3,753[3]	4,830
Occidental	7.21	Dallas, Tex.	3.11	2.41	Group Health Inc.	3,600	4,414
Providence, R.I.	7.37	Birmingham, Ala.	3.28	2.28	San Francisco, Calif.	3,486[3]	4,465
Birmingham, Ala.	7.40	Prudential	3.35	2.81	Prudential	3,121	3,720
Railroad Retirement Board	7.79	Nationwide	3.59	3.00	Jacksonville, Fla.	3,110	3,199
General American	8.02	Concord, N.H.	3.59	2.33	San Juan, P.R.	3,073[3]	3,219
Mutual of Omaha	8.03	General American	3.62	2.82	Nationwide	3,049	3,649
Salt Lake City, Utah	8.27	Boston, Mass.	3.64	2.83	Concord, N.H.	2,990	4,611
Pan American	8.48	R.R.B.	3.67	3.12	Connecticut General	2,968	3,353
Rochester, N.Y.	8.51	Columbia, S.C.	3.82	2.77	Salt Lake City, Utah	2,953	3,830
Indianapolis, Ind.	8.60	Pan American	3.88	2.68	Indianapolis, Ind.	2,949[3]	3,670
New York, N.Y.	8.76	Rochester, N.Y.	3.88	3.35	Birmingham, Ala.	2,944	4,240
Nationwide	9.10	Indianapolis, Ind.	3.95	3.17	New York, N.Y.	2,890[3]	3,597
Boston, Mass.	9.25	San Francisco, Calif.	4.06	3.17	Detroit, Mich.	2,884[3]	3,669

Equitable	9.29	Occidental	4.10	3.64	R.R.B.	2,850	3,352
Chicago, Ill.	9.33	Detroit, Mich.	4.12	3.24	Aetna	2,827	3,132
Washington, D.C.	9.34	Seattle, Wash.	4.13	3.13	Wilmington, Del.	2,805	3,820
Aetna	9.40	Aetna	4.15	3.75	Columbia, S.C.	2,766	3,814
San Juan, P.R.	9.40	Helena, Mont.	4.23	2.98	Pan American	2,751	3,983
Travelers	9.45	Equitable	4.25	3.13	General American	2,741	3,521
Columbia, S.C.	9.81	Little Rock, Ark.	4.26	3.04	Seattle, Wash.	2,726	3,596
Group Health Inc.	9.90	Salt Lake City, Utah	4.29	3.31	Little Rock, Ark.	2,687[3]	3,771
Kansas City, Mo.	10.08	New York, N.Y.	4.30	3.46	Baltimore, Md.	2,675	3,421
Buffalo, N.Y.	10.08	Wilmington, Del.	4.37	3.21	Washington, D.C.	2,656	3,108
Continental Casualty	10.22	Union Mutual	4.38	3.08	Fargo, N. Dak.	2,611	3,333
Little Rock, Ark.	10.50	Group Health Inc.[2]	4.38	3.57	Metropolitan	2,443	2,975
Helena, Mont.	10.51	Baltimore, Md.	4.39	3.43	Equitable	2,436[3]	3,302
Milwaukee, Wis.	10.57	Mutual of Omaha	4.46	3.56	Occidental	2,407[3]	2,712
Sioux Falls, S. Dak.	10.87	Fargo, N. Dak.	4.52	3.54	St. Paul, Minn.	2,389[3]	3,299
Union Mutual	11.00	Milwaukee, Wis.	4.53	3.58	Mutual of Omaha	2,381	2,988
Baltimore, Md.	11.04	Denver, Colo.	4.54	3.33	Helena, Mont.	2,338	3,320
San Francisco, Calif.	11.18	Oklahoma I.S.R.S.	4.73	3.23	Sioux Falls, S. Dak.	2,329[3]	3,020
Concord, N.H.	11.25	Buffalo, N.Y.	4.73	3.50	Denver, Colo.	2,309[3]	3,146
Fargo, N. Dak.	11.34	Metropolitan	4.75	3.90	Topeka, Kans	2,302[3]	3,359
Detroit, Mich.	11.53	Topeka, Kans.	4.77	3.27	Oklahoma I.S.R.S.	2,279	3,338
Seattle, Wash.	11.55	Washington, D.C.	4.93	4.21	Milwaukee, Wis.	2,266	2,864
Metropolitan	11.56	Continental Casualty	5.08	4.45	Union Mutual	2,253	3,199
St. Paul, Minn.	11.76	Travelers	5.09	3.99	Buffalo, N.Y.	2,235	3,018
Wilmington, Del.	11.80	Sioux Falls, S. Dak.	5.09	3.92	Chicago, Ill.	2,178[3]	2,629
Des Moines, Iowa	11.96	Kansas City, Mo.	5.10	4.11	Des Moines, Iowa	2,125[3]	3,094

Table 4-13 (cont.)

Administrative expenses as percentage of benefit payments		Unit cost			Production per man-year bills		
			Payment record	Claim		Payment record	Claim
Topeka, Kans.	12.04	St. Paul, Minn.	5.25	3.81	Continental Casualty	2,120	2,420
Denver, Colo.	12.93	Des Moines, Iowa	5.36	3.68	Travelers	2,008[3]	2,559
Oklahoma I.S.R.S.	15.10	Chicago, Ill.	5.70	4.72	Kansas City, Mo.	1,946	2,418

Source: Unpublished Social Security Administration data.

Notes: 1. Weighted national average.

2. Includes nonrecurring costs.

3. Productivity adjusted to include a manpower equivalent for data-processing costs included without breakouts of manpower or personal services.

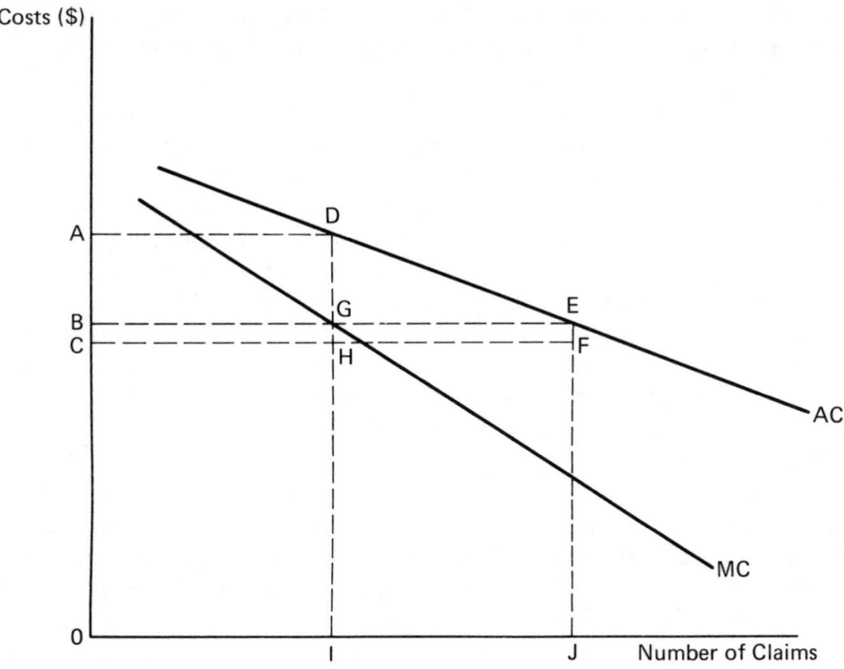

Figure 4-4. Average and Marginal Costs of Administration

administration is then *OADI.* If the firm obtains status as a fiscal agent, the number of claims expands to *OJ.* Because of the presence of economies of scale, average cost falls to *OB.* Total administrative costs are now given by *OBEJ.* Because the *AC* curve includes a normal return on the firm's investment, the firm cannot charge Medicare the full total cost of the Medicare claims, which is represented by *IGEJ.* The rules for reimbursement[8] may only allow a charge to Medicare of *IHFJ.* But as long as *BADG*, the cost saving on its own business, exceeds *HGEF*, the uncompensated portion of total costs due to the Medicare claims, the firm will realize a net cost saving and, therefore, an increase in profits and/or reserves. Thus, it is quite possible that a firm would be more than willing to become a fiduciary under Medicare.

Even though seventy-four of the eighty-three Intermediaries are nonprofit Blue Cross plans and thirty-two of the forty-eight Carriers are Blue Shield plans, the above argument holds equally well for nonprofit firms. As was explained in Chapter 3, the Blues do compete with the commercial companies for customers and even though they enjoy substantial competitive advantages, they should have an incentive to attain technical efficiency. If they can achieve economies of scale by taking on a greater volume of business through the Medicare program, then one would expect them to want to become Intermediaries and Carriers.[i]

In Chapter 3, we found that the Blues have not taken advantage of potential economies of scale in their own business. But there are other reasons for desiring to be a Medicare Intermediary or Carrier: an enhanced marketing position for selling health insurance supplementary to Medicare to the aged; the information on provider costs, which one gains from the audit responsibility, may be carried over to save money in regular business; the opportunity to acquire sophisticated management systems; and the goodwill and prestige engendered by governmental service. A final explanation for fiduciary participation in Medicare comes from the nature of the administrative cost reimbursement method. Consider Figure 4-5. Panel A represents Blue Cross-Blue Shield regular business. AC_1 is the cost function that would prevail were there no Medicare. Because Medicare reimburses all administrative costs, there is no incentive to minimize Medicare administrative costs. In fact, there is a real incentive to maximize Medicare administrative costs subject to the constraints of the rules for reimbursement. If the rules for reimbursement are loosely drawn or loosely interpreted, then some regular business administrative costs might be pushed off onto Medicare administrative costs. For example, on paper, more executive time might be allocated to Medicare than is actually used or the Medicare program might be used as a training program for future regular-business employees. If such practices do occur, then the regular-business cost function would tend to shift downward to AC_2 and this is the cost function that would be observed. In panel B, the observable Medicare cost function would be AC_1. Such an explanation for the transfer of administrative costs between the two segments of business has intuitive appeal for a number of reasons. Lower administrative costs in regular business makes regular business more competitive with commercial health insurance and/or allows more managerial slack for amenities such as plush offices, etc. And, there is no market penalty for having high Medicare administrative costs, especially if everyone else also has them. Further, it is generally conceded that cost or cost-plus reimbursement tends to introduce an invitation to increase costs.[9] And, finally, there is a documentation which lends indirect support to the hypothesis that regular-business costs are transferred to the Medicare program. The staff of the Senate Finance Committee has pointed out that there are some "carve out," reimbursement arrangements between Blue Cross and the hospitals. Under the "carve out" Blue Cross first determines the amount to be paid by the Medicare program and then pays remaining costs for its regular subscribers. By maximizing the Medicare payment to the hospitals, regular-business payments are minimized.[10] If such a practice occurs with

[i]This view implies that Blue Cross-Blue Shield plans try to maximize market share rather than profits.

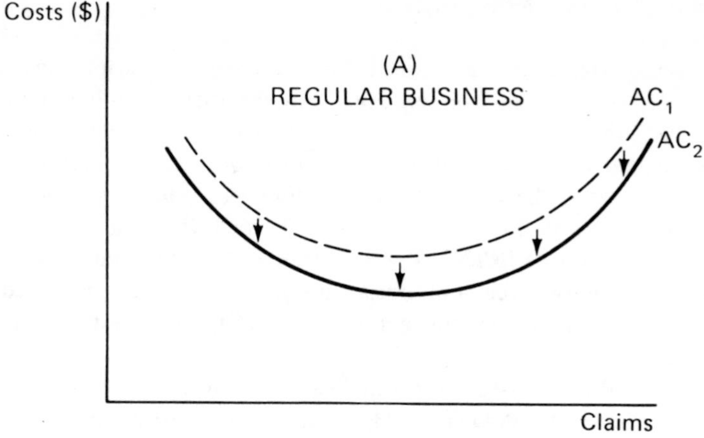

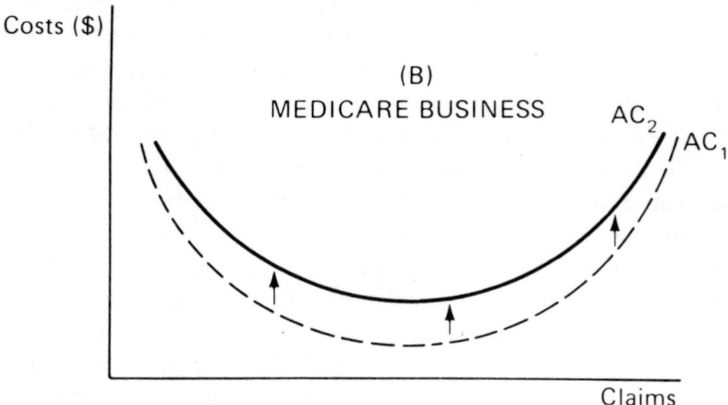

Figure 4-5. Transfer of Costs from Regular Business to Medicare Business

benefit payments, there is no reason to believe that it does not also occur with administrative costs. Indeed, one would expect it to be a common practice because benefit payments are extensively audited under the Medicare program, while administrative costs are not subject to such thorough audits. For these reasons, we expect that our cost estimates for Medicare will not be as successful as they were for the commercial insurers and we have no assurance that the observable Medicare cost function is the true cost function.

Empirical Analysis of Intermediaries

Figure 4-3 indicates that there was a high positive correlation between the percentage of bills received from extended care facilities and unit administrative costs. As was explained in that section of this chapter, this phenomenon is due to a greater amount of adjudication for ECF bills and greater owner and employee turnover in the ECF. Further, the commercial Intermediaries have the highest percentage of ECF bills. It was decided that the payment of a preponderant amount of ECF bills was a different "output" under the Medicare program and, therefore, the commercial Intermediaries are not included in the Medicare regression model in this section of this chapter.[j] The data used are for fiscal 1971.

As with the Blue Cross equation in Chapter 3, we use two concepts of the dependent variable. MOPCOST is Medicare administrative costs divided by Medicare administrative costs plus benefit payments. Because Medicare Part A Intermediaries do not have enrollees, as explained earlier, we could not use a concept similar to ENCOST in the Blue Cross equations in Chapter 3. We, therefore, use MUNCOST which is Medicare administrative costs divided by the number of Medicare bills. The Social Security Administration provides a breakdown of administrative costs by provider audit costs and all administrative costs other than provider audit costs. To ascertain if our independent variables could explain variations in these two components of administrative costs, we also used as dependent variables MAUCOST, which is provider audit costs divided by Medicare benefits paid, and MADCOST, which is all administrative costs other than provider audit costs divided by Medicare benefits paid.

As with the commercials and Blues under their regular business, we might expect the size of the firm to make a difference in operating costs. Because the size variable had no effect under regular Blue Cross business, we expect that it will not affect Medicare business operating results either. Accordingly, we include the SIZE variable, defined, as previously, as total claims under all lines of business. Given the finding of economies of scale for commercial insurers in Chapter 2, but given the fact that we could find no economies of scale for Blue Cross regular business in Chapter 3, we have no a priori way of knowing what the sign of the SIZE variable will be in the Medicare equations, nor can we be sure that the SIZE variable will be significant. If administrative cost "carving out" does occur, a positive sign on SIZE would indicate that the larger Blue Cross Intermediaries are more efficient at "carving out." Of course, a negative sign on SIZE would indicate the opposite.

We would expect some economies from specialization and therefore include the independent variable MEDCARE. This variable measures Medicare claims as

[j]When a regression model including the commercials and the ECF variables was run, the ECF variable so swamped the other independent variables that the results were open to questionable interpretation.

a percentage of total claims. To the extent that an Intermediary specializes in handling Medicare claims, we would expect the coefficient on this variable to be negative. For the same reason, we have used the Federal Employees Plan claims as a percentage of total claims. To the extent that an Intermediary handles the large *uniform* FEP program, it should be more efficient in dealing with Medicare because the FEP program is similar to Medicare. Accordingly, we would expect the sign of the coefficient on FEP to be negative.

Labor market conditions vary around the country, as do the cost of living and levels of education of the labor force. General wage variables are not very helpful, however, since Medicare employees must be more highly skilled. Thus, we have used the average Medicare employee salary (AMES) to capture this effect. The average size of a claim also ought to have an effect upon the level of operating costs, although this effect will differ depending upon which definition of the dependent variable is used. If the cost of administering a claim does not rise as rapidly as the amount of the claim, then we would expect MACS (Medicare average claim size) to be signed negatively vis-à-vis MOPCOST. When MUNCOST is the dependent variable, we would expect the sign of MACS to be positive even if the cost of administering a claim does not rise as rapidly as the amount of the claim. Larger claims should demand more labor time and processing, driving up MUNCOST. But, because of the fact that the amount of the claim size is contained in the denominator of MOPCOST, larger claims should lower MOPCOST.

The number of claims submitted by the providers of medical care to the aged also ought to influence the level of operating costs. We, therefore, have used CLPROV, the number of claims per provider, as an independent variable. The sign of the coefficient of this variable ought to be negative because the more claims submitted per provider the more provider specialization in bill submission possible and we would, therefore, expect less errors in billing. Finally, extended care facility bills are more expensive to administer than hospital bills and so we include the variable PROPECF which is the proportion of Medicare bills which come from the ECF. The sign of the coefficient on this variable should be positive.

These were thought to be the most important factors explaining variations in the administrative costs of the intermediaries. The basic form of the regression model is:

$$\begin{aligned}\text{Dependent Variable}_i = {} & b_0 + b_1\text{SIZE}_i + b_2\text{SIZE}_i^2 + b_3\text{MEDICARE}_i \\ & + b_4\text{FEP}_i + b_5\text{AMES}_i + b_6\text{MACS}_i \\ & + b_7\text{CLPROV}_i + b_8\text{PROPECF}_i + u_i . \qquad (4.1)\end{aligned}$$

To estimate this relationship, we used unpublished data collected by the Social Security Administration. The regression results are presented in Table 4-14.

Table 4-14
Medicare Part A Regression Results*

	CONSTANT	SIZE	QSIZE	MEDCARE	FEP	MACS	AMES	CLPROV	PROPECF	$\bar{R}^2$	Sy
MOPCOST	.215 –01 (5.33)	.212 –05 (1.829)	–.180 –09 (.784)	.214 –04 (.595)	.300 –03 (3.202)	–.354 –01 (4.840)	.172 –05 (1.153)	–.702 –06 (1.511)	.372 –02 (.139)	33	.003
	.213 –01 (5.309)	.131 –06 (2.501)		.168 –04 (.477)	.304 –03 (3.273)	–.347 –01 (4.798)	.196 –05 (1.351)	–.703 –06 (1.517)	.473 –02 (.177)	.34	003
	.203 –01 (4.873)			–.170 –04 (.499)	.293 –03 (3.017)	–.264 –01 (3.932)	.236 –06 (1.576)	–.833 –06 (1.731)	.849 –02 (.305)	.28	.004
MUNCOST	.287 –02 (2.395)	.764 –06 (2.217)	–.808 –10 (1.187)	.136 –05 (.127)	.796 –04 (2.864)	.412 –02 (1.895)	.174 –06 (.393)	–.242 –06 (1.751)	.176 –02 (.222)	.32	.001
	.277 –02 (2.307)	.399 –06 (2.545)		–.683 –06 (.065)	.183 –04 (2.940)	.442 –02 (2.042)	.284 –06 (.652)	–.242 –06 (1.746)	.222 –02 (.278)	.32	.001
	.248 –02 (1.980)			–.110 –04 (1.076)	.783 –04 (2.690)	.695 –02 (3.443)	.410 –06 (.907)	–.282 –06 (1.953)	.336 –02 (.404)	.25	.001
MAUCOST	.338 –.02 (1.706)	.833 –06 (1.465)	–.100 –09 (.892)	.267 –04 (1.516)	.138 –03 (3.007)	–.311 –02 (.868)	.359 –06 (.490)	–.732 –06 (3.206)	.182 –01 (1.388)	.29	.002
MADCOST	.185 –01 (5.472)	.135 –05 (1.386)	–.831 –10 (.433)	–.399 –05 (.133)	.173 –03 (2.204)	–.335 –01 (5.460)	.145 –05 (1.162)	.501 –08 (.013)	–.141 –01 (.627)	.30	.003

*Results are based upon 64 observations. The *t*-values are in parentheses.

The regression results are a bit disappointing because none of the regression models explains more than 34 percent of the variation in Medicare administration costs.[k] As in the Blue Cross regular business equations, the SIZE variable has a positive sign and is statistically significant at conventional levels. There are at least two ways of interpreting the sign of the coefficient on the SIZE variable. The first interpretation would imply that "carving out" does occur and that the larger Blue Cross intermediaries are more efficient at "carving out" than the smaller Blue Cross intermediaries. For this interpretation to be completely convincing, however, the coefficient on the SIZE variable in the regular business equations would have to be negative; that coefficient was not negative. One might still argue that "carving" occurs under Medicare and that the larger Blue Cross plans still have higher costs than the smaller Blue Cross plans in their regular business because of more favorable treatment vis-à-vis their commercial competition. This argument is simply less convincing. The second interpretation of the positive sign on the SIZE coefficient is that large intermediaries are less efficient than small intermediaries. This interpretation is difficult to accept because of findings of economies of scale in other studies of other parts of the insurance industry. Clearly, further research must be done on this issue. The Medicare average claim size variable, MACS, has the expected sign, positive in the MUNCOST equations, and negative in the MOPCOST equations and is statistically significant at the .01 level. Also of interest is the fact that MACS is not significant in the MAUCOST equation. This also is to be expected because the provider audit function is not related to the claims process. The coefficients of CLPROV and AMES have the expected sign but lack statistical significance in most equations. The coefficient of FEP has a sign opposite of that expected and its *t* value indicates that there is no reason to believe that the value of its coefficient is zero. In general, the coefficients of MEDCARE and PROPECF are of the expected sign but are not statistically significant.

Empirical Analysis of Carriers

As in the Medicare Part A equations, we used MOPCOST and MUNCOST as dependent variables. Furthermore, because Medicare Part B carriers do service definite geographical areas, one may properly say that they do have enrollees. Therefore, we also used Medicare administrative costs per enrollee (MENCOST) as a dependent variable.

We include SIZE and size squared, QSIZE, with the expectation that the size of the Carrier would make a difference in the level of administrative

[k]Provider characteristics such as average bed size, percentage state and local hospitals, percentage teaching hospitals, and patient characteristics such as percentage over age 75, percentage black, percentage below the poverty line were also used in regressions not presented here. Results using these independent variables were equally disappointing.

costs. Again, though, given past experience with this variable in the Blue Cross-Blue Shield equations we are pessimistic about its efficacy in explaining variations in administrative costs.[l]

Due to the possibility of fraud in the Medicare payment process, it is necessary to investigate the validity of a certain proportion of the claims submitted for payment. Since such investigation adds to the administrative costs[m] of the program, one would expect that the higher the percentage of bills investigated (PBI), the higher a Carrier's administrative costs would be relative to other Carriers.

The Carriers number among their ranks both nonprofit Blue Shield plans and profit-seeking commercial firms. Since it would be of some interest to know whether there is any difference between their respective operating costs, we have included firm type. We used a dummy variable (COMM), which takes on the value one if the firm is a commercial Carrier and zero otherwise. Although any a priori expectations as to the sign of the coefficient on COMM is open to argument, we felt that a profit-seeking firm would be more likely to minimize costs. Thus, we anticipated a negative coefficient on COMM. Because some of the commercial Carriers handle Medicare claims in two or three states with payment centers in each state, we used a dummy variable (MPC) which takes on a value of one for the payment centers of those commercials and zero otherwise. We have no way of knowing what the sign of the coefficient of this variable will be.

The size of the claims that the Carrier pays ought to affect its level of operating costs. As in the intermediary equations, we used the Medicare average claim size (MACS) as the dependent variable. In the MOPCOST equations its coefficient should be negative and in the MUNCOST equations positive for the same reasons outlined in the intermediary empirical analysis. The more claims submitted per provider the more specialization in billing possible. Thus, we include number of claims per physician (CLPROV) as an independent variable. The coefficient on this variable ought to be negative.

Physicians may accept assignment of payment of bills directly from the Carrier. If the physician does not accept assignment, the elderly person must pay the physician bill himself and then submit a claim to the Carrier for reimbursement. To the extent that the physician submits bills on which he has accepted assignment, the bills would have been either filed by him or a member of his office staff. Accordingly, one might expect that assigned bills would have a

[l]The definition of this SIZE variable is different than in the other equations because we have no data on regular business claims of the commercial carriers. Accordingly, we used benefits paid under the Medicare program as the SIZE variable.

[m]Although such investigations must add to the *administrative* costs of Medicare, investigations tend to reduce the *claims* costs of the program. Clearly, investigations should be increased until the marginal reduction in fraudulent claims is equal to the marginal cost of increasing the number of investigations. It would be of some interest to determine whether this optimality rule is used.

greater probability of being correct than unassigned bills and cause less work for the Carrier. We, therefore, included the percentage of claims that were assigned (ASSIGN) as an independent variable and expect its sign to be negative.

Presently, the Carriers are using four different types of data processing systems. These have been designated by the Social Security Administration, as "own system" (OWNSYS), "model system" (DELSYS), "Applied Systems Development Corporation" (ASDC), and "electronic data processing system" (EDS). The "model system" has been recommended by the Social Security Administration as the system that will insure the most satisfactory handling of claims. We included dummy variables DELSYS, OWNSYS, and ASDC in the regression equation to determine the effects of the different data processing systems on unit costs.[11]

Finally, we would expect the level of wages to have some effect upon per unit administrative costs. Thus, we have used the average Medicare employee salary (AMES) as an explanatory variable. Clearly, one would expect a positive coefficient. The form of the regression model is:

$$\begin{aligned}\text{Dependent Variable}_i = {} & b_0 + b_1\text{SIZE}_i + b_2\text{QSIZE}_i + b_3\text{COMM}_i \\ & + b_4\text{MPC}_i + b_5\text{MACS}_i + b_6\text{CLPROV}_i \\ & + b_7\text{ASSGN}_i + b_8\text{PBI}_i + b_9\text{DELSYS}_i \\ & + b_{10}\text{OWNSYS}_i + b_{11}\text{ASDC}_i \\ & + b_{12}\text{AMES}_i + u_i. \end{aligned} \tag{4.2}$$

The regression results are contained in Table 4-15. The variables SIZE and QSIZE do not affect the dependent variable when MOPCOST and MUNCOST are used. SIZE and QSIZE, however, are statistically significant in the MENCOST equation. This, of course, indicates that the SIZE relationship is curvilinear. Of interest is the fact that the COMM variable is consistently negative,[12] indicating that the commercial Carriers have lower administrative costs than the Blue Shield Carriers, but this result is not statistically significant, except in one of the equations. MACS also has the expected sign, and is statistically significant in most of the equations. CLPROV has the expected sign but is not statistically significant. ASSIGN does not have the expected sign, nor is it statistically significant, while AMES performed well in explaining all three concepts of the dependent variable. The evidence is rather mixed with respect to the data processing systems. The signs and the statistical significance of the coefficients are not stable. Thus, any inference would be extremely tentative.[13]

Conclusions

We have found that when administrative costs are expressed as a percentage of benefits paid or on a per enrollee basis, Medicare Part B has proved to be more

Table 4-15
Medicare Part B Regression Results*

	CONSTANT	SIZE	QSIZE	PBI	COMM	MPC	MACS	CLPROV	ASSIGN	DELSYS	OWNSYS	ASDC	AMES	$\bar{R}^2$	Sy
MOPCOST	.943 −01 (3.191)	−.143 −07 (1.647)	.303 −14 (1.514)	.994 −03 (1.266)	−.193 −03 (.028)	−.447 −02 (.602)	−.119 +01 (3.399)	−.693 −05 (.465)	−.413 −04 (.210)	−.424 −03 (.047)	−.240 −02 (.295)	−.140 −01 (1.081)	.664 −5 (1.957)	.23	.017
	.981 −01 (3.285)	−.217 −08 (.640)		.856 −03 (1.083)	−.303 −02 (.445)	−.787 −02 (1.097)	−.136 +01 (4.000)	−.863 −05 (.574)	−.935 −04 (.477)	.617 −03 (.068)	−.102 −02 (.125)	−.135 −01 (1.024)	.733 −05 (2.149)	.21	.017
	.103 +00 (3.566)			.903 −03 (1.154)	−.376 −02 (.564)	−.857 −02 (1.217)	−.141 +01 (4.338)	−.120 −04 (.859)	−.121 −03 (.637)	.375 −02 (.493)	.176 −02 (.255)	−.966 −02 (.829)	.670 −05 (2.064)	.21	.017
MUNCOST	.619 −03 (.510)	−.561 −09 (1.576)	.113 −15 (1.369)	.230 −04 (.712)	−.107 −03 (.373)	−.126 −03 (.414)	.388 −01 (2.686)	−.444 −06 (.727)	−.172 −05 (.214)	.139 −04 (.377)	−.921 −04 (.276)	−.595 −03 (1.117)	.277 −06 (1.982)	.31	.001
	.759 −03 (.621)	−.111 −09 (.804)		.178 −04 (.552)	−.213 −03 (.762)	−.253 −03 (.861)	.327 −01 (2.360)	−.508 −06 (.825)	−.366 −05 (.457)	.178 −03 (.478)	−.408 −04 (.122)	−.575 −03 (1.068)	.302 −06 (2.164)	.29	.001
	.996 −03 (.843)			.202 −04 (.630)	−.250 −03 (.913)	−.289 −03 (1.000)	.299 −01 (2.236)	−.682 −06 (1.188)	−.507 −05 (.651)	.339 −03 (1.086)	.102 −03 (.361)	−.379 −03 (.793)	.269 −06 (2.025)	.30	.001
MENCOST	−.106 −02 (.319)	−.215 −08 (2.216)	.102 −14 (4.531)	.141 −03 (1.603)	−.123 −02 (1.576)	−.825 −03 (.991)	−.339 −02 (.086)	−.365 −06 (.218)	.148 −04 (.674)	.216 −02 (2.137)	.978 −03 (1.072)	.842 −03 (.578)	.110 −05 (2.899)	.57	.002
	.203 −03 (.052)	.191 −08 (4.281)		.949 −04 (.911)	−.219 −02 (2.439)	−.197 −02 (2.083)	−.579 −01 (1.296)	−.938 −06 (.473)	−.269 −05 (.104)	.251 −02 (2.093)	.144 −02 (1.337)	.103 −02 (.594)	.134 −05 (2.971)	.40	.002
	−.386 −02 (.867)			.541 −04 (.447)	−.155 −02 (1.497)	−.135 −02 (1.238)	−.847 −02 (.168)	.205 −05 (.945)	.214 −04 (.730)	−.255 −03 (.216)	−.101 −02 (.246)	−.232 −02 (1.289)	.189 −05 (3.775)	.18	.003

*Results based upon 59 observations. The *t*-values are in parentheses.

expensive to administer than Part A. In contrast, however, administrative costs per bill have been lower under Part B. This seeming paradox is resolved by recognizing that average benefits per bill paid under Part A have been three times those paid under Part B. The apparent paradox serves to illustrate the hazards of making comparisons on a ratio basis without a careful analysis of underlying factors.

Between 1967 and 1968, benefit payments on a per enrollee basis increased at a more rapid rate than administrative costs and the most rapid increase in these two items occurred between 1967 and 1968. The large percentage increase between those two years reflects the considerable lag before bills were submitted and processed for reimbursement. Since then, the administrative system has had time to consolidate itself and rates of increases have been fairly constant. If one uses 1968 as a base, he finds that administrative costs per enrollee have increased at a more rapid rate than benefits per enrollee. This phenomenon is due to benefit lags in 1967 and increased expenditures for monitoring the program that simultaneously increased administrative costs and produced a consequent relative reduction in claims paid. Indeed, provider audit and claims review per bill have been the most rapidly growing administrative expenditures under the Part A program. Such expenditures are designed to enhance overall program quality even though they do drive up administrative costs. Part B administrative costs per claim have remained relatively stable, despite increased labor costs, due to the fact that Part B bills more easily lend themselves to electronic data processing and because provider audits and claims review are not required under the Part B program.

Medicare business accounts for a significant percentage of Intermediary and Carrier business especially for Blue Cross and Blue Shield. The reasons why an insurer would want to be a Medicare Intermediary or Carrier were given and then we tested empirical models of Intermediary and Carrier cost behavior. As with Blue Cross-Blue Shield regular business, we did not find evidence of economies of scale in their Medicare business with the exception of one Blue Shield equation. Our regression results were disappointing but, again, do give some credence to our theory of nonprofit behavior expounded in Chapter 3. We also could not find evidence of "carving out" but we could not find evidence against it either. Given experience with other forms of cost reimbursement, however, the presupposition exists that it does occur. Certainly, the intermediaries and carriers do not have ncentives to minimize administrative costs. The incentive is in the opposite direction, particularly in the absence of any competition.

From a policy point of view, high administrative costs are not necessarily undesirable. The efficient insurer would spend money on administrative costs up to the point where the marginal dollar for administrative costs would just equal the marginal dollar saved on unjustified benefit payments.

Notes

1. Social Security Bulletin, March 1974, Tables M-7 and M-8, pp. 52-53.

2. Cf. *Age Patterns in Medicare Care, Illness and Disability–United States July 1963-June 1965*, U.S. Department of Health, Education and Welfare, Public Health Service, National Center for Health Statistics, Series 10, No. 32 (1966), Table 1.

3. Barbara S. Cooper and Nancy L. Worthington, "Age Differences in Medical Care Spending," Fiscal Year 1972, *Social Security Bulletin*, May 1973.

4. See John Krizay, "Does the Social Security Administration Really Run Medicare on Two Percent of Income?" *Perspective*, Fourth Quarter, 1972, pp. 12-16 and inserted in the *Congressional Record*, June 7, 1973, p. F10602. John Krizay, "Health Insurance: Can the Government Do It Cheaper?" *Bests Review*, January 1973, p. 15.

5. B.J. Weiss, et al., "Trends in Health Insurance Operating Expenses," *New England Journal of Medicine*, September 28, 1972, pp. 638-642.

6. For a more detailed analysis of this phenomenon see, Howard West, "Five Years of Medicare–A Statistical Review," *Social Security Bulletin*, December 1971.

7. Barbara S. Cooper and Nancy L. Worthington, "Medical Care Outlays for Three Age Groups," *Social Security Bulletin*, May 1971, and Barbara S. Cooper and Nancy L. Worthington, "Age Differences in Medical Care Spending, Fiscal Year 1972," *Social Security Bulletin*, May 1973.

8. The actual rules for reimbursement are spelled out in some detail in Chapter 1, "Principles of Reimbursement for Administrative Costs of U.S. Department of Health, Education and Welfare, Social Security Administration," *Health Insurance for the Aged, Part I, Administration, Part B Intermediary Manual*, HIM 14-1 (8-67), Reprint Date (4-72).

9. See Robert Perry et al., *System Acquisition Strategies*, R-733-PR/ARPA, RAND Corporation, June 1971. M.J. Peck and F.M. Scherer, *The Weapons Acquisition Process: An Economic Analysis* (Cambridge: Harvard University Press, 1962). F.M. Scherer, *The Weapons Acquisition Process: Economic Incentives* (Cambridge: Harvard University Press, 1964). Comptroller General of the United States General Accounting Office, *Acquisition of Major Weapon Systems*, March 18, 1971. Frederick M. Scherer, "The Aerospace Industry," in Walter Adams (ed.), *The Structure of American Industry* (New York: The Macmillan Company, 1971), pp. 335-379. Frederick T. Moore, *Military Procurement and Contracting: An Economic Analysis*, RAND Corporation, RM-2948-PR, 1962. Hearings before the Subcommittee on Priorities and Economy in Government of the Joint Economic Committee, Congress of the United States, *The Acquisition of Weapons Systems*, Part 7, November 14, 15, and 16, 1973.

10. Staff Report, Senate Finance Committee, *Medicare and Medicaid: Prob-*

lems, Issues and Alternatives (Washington: U.S. Government Printing Office, February 9, 1970), p. 116.

11. Formulated in this fashion, the coefficients on DELSYS, OWNSYS, and ASDC measure the differential effects of the "model system" the "own system" and the "Applied Systems Development Corporation" system against those Carriers using the "EDS" system. For a further discussion of dummy variables, cf., J. Johnston, *Econometric Methods*, 2nd ed. (New York: McGraw-Hill, 1972), pp. 180-181.

12. Indeed, a property rights theory of the firm would have predicted this outcome. Because the decision maker in a for-profit firm has residual property rights in the outcome of the competitive process, he has a strong incentive to make his firm efficient. The decision maker in the nonprofit firm has no property rights and, therefore, has less incentive to be efficient. See David M. Barton and H.E. "Ted" Frech, III, "The Property Rights Theory of the Firm: Empirical Results From a Natural Experiment," University of California, Santa Barbara, Department of Economics, Working Papers in Economics #28, May 1974.

13. As with the Part A equations, provider characteristic variables and patient characteristic variables were tried in regressions not reported here. These variables provided no additional explanatory power. The generally low R^2 and lack of statistical significance of the explanatory variables are consistent with the findings of the "Perkins Committee." See *Report to the Secretary of HEW and the Commissioner of the Social Security Administration* by the Advisory Committee on Medicare Administration, Contracting, and Subcontracting, June 21, 1974, U.S. Department of Health, Education and Welfare, MAGS-2 (6-74). The Perkins Committee expressed surprise at the wide variability in Medicare Part B administrative costs. We have found that Medicare Part B administrative costs vary much less than Blue Shield regular business costs.

5 Summary and Conclusions

This study analyzes the administrative cost experience of the three largest health insuring entities in the United States: (1) the commercial insurers, (2) Blue Cross-Blue Shield, and (3) the federal government's Medicare program. For purposes of discussing which form a national health insurance system should assume, it is tempting to compare the administrative cost experience of the three different entities and to make statements about their respective efficiencies or inefficiencies. We have found, however, that the commonly used measures for comparison are inappropriate and misleading if not used with extreme caution. The most common practice is to use some ratio such as administrative expenses as a percentage of premiums written or earned, or administrative expenses as a percentage of benefits paid. In using such a ratio, the individual making the comparison implicitly assumes that the health insurance service (or the "product" or "output") being provided by the three major entities is homogeneous. While such an assumption may be close to the truth when comparing the output of, say, differing steel companies, it is generally invalid for the service sector of the economy and for the health insurance industry in particular.[1]

In an actuarially "fair" world, i.e., where there were no selling costs, no administrative costs, and no other services provided, on average for each individual over time, health premiums paid would exactly equal benefits received because the individual would be buying pure protection against the incidence of morbidity and its treatment. In a world where the individual is buying other services along with pure health insurance protection, premiums paid must be greater than benefits received on average over time. This follows because a portion of the premium must be used to pay for the other services that the individual is purchasing along with his pure health insurance protection. When a ratio comparison is made of differing insuring entities and statements about efficiency are based on that comparison, the fact that the insuring entities may be offering a variety of different services is totally ignored. Thus, such comparisons are conceptually invalid for the purpose of comparing efficiency in delivering health insurance.

A further difficulty in the use of the above-mentioned ratios arises from the fact that the ratio lends itself to a type of manipulation. Recall the following equation:

$$B = P - (A + C),$$

where B represents a break-even point or a targeted level of profit, P denotes premiums, A is administrative costs, and C is claims costs. Clearly, the firm can obtain a constant value for B by lowering A and increasing C by equal amounts. There are any number of reasons why an insuring organization might allow such offsetting changes. For example, the firm may find that a reduction in the claims review process, which lowers A, will be accompanied by an increase in claims costs just offsetting the saving in administrative costs. Since profitability is unchanged, the firm is indifferent between the alternatives and may hope to gain customer goodwill. Comparing the ratio $\frac{A}{P}$ or $\frac{A}{C}$ on a before and after basis would make the above health insuring organization appear to be more efficient after it had let A and C increase. Actually, there would be no change in efficiency because its claims review function would have deteriorated, but its claims payment function expanded.[a] Therefore, if the analyst uses ratios when comparing *different types* of health insurers, he must proceed with even greater caution. We have used such ratios at many points in this study and can only hope we have exercised enough care to use them correctly.

In proceeding with the empirical analysis, we treated the three major providers of health insurance (the commercials, Blue Cross-Blue Shield, and Medicare) separately because of the large difference in the types of services that they provide beyond the provision of pure health insurance protection. In Table 5-1, a functional enumeration of these differing services is provided for the reader. Perusal of this enumeration illustrates the difficulty, perhaps the impossibility, of making statements about the relative efficiency of the three major providers of health insurance. Because the Medicare clientele is beyond the age of sixty-five, a vast informational network is required to explain to the aged their rights and obligations under the program; a more youthful population would probably need less attention from administrators of the program. Besides its health insurance function, Medicare also performs a civil rights function and a provider quality-certification function. In many respects, Blue Cross-Blue Shield currently resembles the commercial carriers in the way it operates and in the functions it performs. The major differences between the two organizations are that the preponderant amount of health insurance which Blue Cross-Blue Shield sells is group health insurance, and the commercial insurers maintain a vast sales force that goes out into the market and searches for customers, particularly in the case of individual health insurance. The Blues also pay a negligible amount of premium taxes to the states, whereas the commercials pay premium taxes which amount to a little more than 2 percent of all premiums written. It has been said that the sales network performs a useful function in that it searches out and

[a]The fact that some unjustified claims are paid is unfortunate. As long as claims review is not free, however, the *optimal* number of unjustified, but paid, claims is not zero. In economic terms, claims review should be pursued until its incremental cost is just equal to the savings in claims payments. Of course, political considerations may easily lead to an overinvestment in claims review.

provides protection for those who would not otherwise obtain health insurance. The commercials and the Blues may also perform a useful function regarding consumer choice since they offer a variety of coverages, which a uniform plan such as Medicare cannot do.

Our analysis of the commercial health insurers is based largely upon a sample of 327 health insurers for the period 1968-1970. Our most important finding is that there are economies of scale in the administration of commercial health insurance. We showed that as firms become larger, their administrative cost ratio falls. This is particularly true when large amounts of group health insurance are sold. There is also some reason to believe that the administrative costs of mutual companies differ materially from those of stock companies. The cost of administering commercial health insurance appears to vary widely depending upon (1) whether the insurance is group or individual and (2) the volume of insurance written by the company. Individual insurance, with its high selling costs, is much more expensive to administer than group insurance. Indeed, in our sample, the median administrative cost ratio for group health insurance was 18.8 percent, while the comparable figure for individual health insurance was 47.0 percent, or 150 percent greater than for group health insurance. A smaller sample of the largest health insurance companies, taken from the *Annual Statement* filed at the offices of the District of Columbia Insurance Commission, reveals why there is such a striking difference in cost ratios: while commissions on group health average only 2.7 percent of premiums, on most forms of individual health coverage commissions average around 20 percent. General insurance expenses are also much higher for individual than for group health insurance. An analysis of variance applied to the smaller sample indicates that there is no systematic difference in the commission structure of the largest members of the commercial health insurance industry, while comparable analyses of variance applied to total administrative expenses and general insurance operating expenses also indicate no systematic differences.

Another way of examining administrative costs is to view them over time. During the period 1965-1970, *commercial* health insurance administrative expenses per insuree increased at an average annual rate of 5.1 percent, while premiums earned and claims costs per insuree increased at average annual rates of 6.0 percent and 7.5 percent, respectively. The slower rate of increase in administrative costs is to be expected because the factors affecting inflation in administering the insurance industry are markedly different from those affecting inflation in the medical care market.

Our empirical results explain, in part, the structure of the commercial health insurance industry. The twenty-six largest insurers write 70 percent and 40 percent, respectively, of the group and individual commercial health business while the smaller, high-cost firms have the rest. This type of industry structure is consistent with economies of scale. If there are large economies of scale in the provision of health insurance, then it seems difficult to explain how the small

Table 5-1
Comparison of Administrative Activities of the Three Major Providers of Health Insurance[1]

Description	Medicare	Blue Cross-Blue Shield and Commercial Insurers	
		Group Plans	Individual Insurance
Enrollment	Determination of eligibility based on age and insured status under social security. Information activities directed toward aged population with relatively low educational background. Individual enrollment under Part A and individual voluntary enrollment under Part B.	Performed by employer through the personnel office. No eligibility requirements. Employee easy to reach. Plans tailored to each individual employer's particular needs and requirements.	Extensive network of sales personnel who sell policies, maintain them andprovide aid to insuree in the claims process. Large amount of resources devoted to information activities such as advertising. Large variety of kinds of protection offered to insurees.
Collection of premiums	Individual collection of Part B premium from persons not receiving cash benefits.	Payroll deductions, at expense of employer.	Insuree is billed annually or semi-annually for the insurance which will be provided to him.
Assistance to claimants	Assistance provided through social security office for enrollment and claims to aged population.	Provided by employer ot by mail.	Provided by mail or by salesman, brokers or agents.
Certification of providers	Enforcement of provisions designed to assure health, safety and quality of care, applies to hospitals, nursing homes, diagnostic laboratories, and other providers.	Enrollment of participating providers by Blues. No enforcement powers.	Enrollment of participating providers by Blues. No enforcement powers.
Scrutinizing of claims	Maintain profiles of physicians' fee.	Some companies beginning to maintain physician fee and provider charge profiles. Blues apparently more active in this area than commercial insurers.	Some companies beginning to maintain physician fee and provider charge files. Blues apparently more active in this area than commercial insurers.

Civil Rights	Enforcement of Civil Rights provisions (Title VI of 1964 Act) for providers of service, carriers and intermediaries.	Obliged to adhere to Civil Rights provisions of Title VI of 1964 Act.	Obliged to adhere to Civil Rights provisions of Title VI of 1964 Act.
Records and reports	Necessity for public accountability requires considerable reporting.	Necessary for internal purposes, tax purposes, and State regulatory agencies. Annual statement must be filed in each State where business is done. Blues must justify rate increases to State insurance commissions.	Necessary for internal purposes, tax purposes, and State regulatory agencies. Annual statement must be filed in each State where business is done. Blues must justify rate increases to State insurance commissions.
Evaluation and research	Continuous study and evaluation of programs. General research in area of medical care costs and delivery.	Commercial insurers participate in a number of associations such as the Health Insurance Association of America and the Health Insurance Institute which publish comparative data and follow industry trends. Blue Cross-Blue Shield collects data at national headquarters and disseminates comparative data to member plans.	Commercial insurers participate in a number of associations such as the Health Insurance Association of America and the Health Insurance Institute which publish comparative data and follow industry trends. Blue Cross-Blue Shield collects data at national headquarters and disseminates comparative data to member plans.
Personnel practices	Cooperation with national policy to hire the handicapped and special efforts to hire the disadvantaged.	Variable among carriers.	Variable among carriers.
Public policy	Acts as agent in enforcement of Price Commission regulations.	Blues provide a certain amount of income redistribution by using community rating. Commercial insurers and Blues provide insurance for certain individuals and groups who would otherwise lack protection.	Blues provide a certain amount of income redistribution by using community rating. Commercial insurers and Blues provide insurance for certain individuals and groups who would otherwise lack protection.

Note:
1. This schema is based upon some previous work by Saul Waldman of the Office of Research and Statistics, Social Security Administration.

high-cost companies can remain in business. One possible explanation is that consumers are atomized, insurance packages are difficult to understand, and no form of unit pricing exists. Thus, the market for individual insurance and small group plans can easily become a sellers market where a large amount of product differentiation occurs and price per "unit of insurance" is incomprehensible and becomes a secondary factor in the evaluation of the product being sold. Reliance is placed upon a large sales force that seeks out individuals and small groups and creates or finds a health insurance package tailor-made to suit the "needs" of the small group or individual. The high commission structure is suggestive that health insurance protection is not always an easy service to sell. Larger purchasers of group health insurance, on the other hand, are more sophisticated, have specialists who can seek out the large, low-cost commercial health insurance companies, and know exactly what they are buying. In general, non-price competition is at least partially offsetting and product differentiation is one such form of non-price competition that can be, and possibly is, overdone.

Ultimately, the question of whether there is too much product proliferation by the commercial health insurers reduces itself to the question of consumer sovereignty: if the multiplicity of policies offered actually hinders freedom of consumer choice and confuses the consumer, then the outcome of the competitive process in the health insurance industry has been inefficient in the provision of health insurance because of increased claims-handling and selling costs. Moreover, it is inefficient in the consumption of health insurance because of consumer befuddlement. If, on the other hand, consumers actually want and need a large variety of health insurance protection, then the commercial insurers are offering a valuable service whose price enters into their administrative costs, thus making their costs *appear* higher than the costs for the services of the Blues or Medicare.

Chapter 3 contains the analysis of the administrative costs of Blue Cross and Blue Shield. In that chapter, we directed most of our attention to the Blues' regular business. Because the Blue Cross plans primarily provide hospital insurance while Blue Shield deals with medical-surgical protection, we analyzed each one separately.

We used two concepts of average administrative costs for the Blue Cross-Blue Shield operations. First, we used total administrative costs divided by benefits paid plus administrative costs. The second measure was total administrative costs divided by the total number of enrollees. The explanatory variables fell into two main categories: size-related variables and product-mix variables. Using the number of claims paid as an indicator of size, we estimated cost functions with the size variable entered linearly and quadratically. Given our results for the commercial health insurers, we fully expected to find some indication of scale economies. In fact, we have not found the presence of scale economies. This result led us to suspect that the nonprofit status of the Blues' may offer an explanation. In other words, the nonprofit organizational form has not resulted in cost minimizing behavior on the part of the Blues. This result is at odds with most theories of the firm that consider alternatives to profit-maximizing behavior. In most formulations, there is always an incentive to minimize costs in the pursuit of maximizing the objective function. The only explanation for not minimizing costs lies in managerial slack, which means primarily not requiring enough output from any given set of inputs. Support for this hypothesis comes from two sources: an analysis of Blue Cross-Blue Shield performance under Medicare and an analysis of potential economies in Blue Cross-Blue Shield mergers.

The rules for reimbursing Intermediaries and Carriers for work performed on behalf of the Medicare program are quite detailed. If substantial managerial slack characterizes the operations of Blue Cross and Blue Shield, then the Blues' administrative costs incurred in their regular business should not correlate well with those costs incurred in performing their Medicare responsibilities. Moreover, one should expect greater variation in the private administrative costs. Our regression analysis yields results that support the notion that substantial managerial slack exists. We find virtually no relationship between the administrative costs incurred in pursuit of the Blues' regular business and those incurred on behalf of Medicare. In addition, the variance of their own costs is substantially greater than the variance of the administrative costs for the Medicare business.

Although we have found some supporting evidence for the hypothesis that managerial slack exists, we looked for further support in the evolution of the Blues' organizational form. Specifically, one would expect that economies could be achieved by merging Blue Cross and Blue Shield in areas where they operate simultaneously. The reason for the supposed economies lies in the economies of scale that could be achieved in the computerized operations plus the removal of duplication in the executive suite and in advertising. By estimating the same cost function as before and using a dummy variable for the effectively merged operation, we could focus on the effect of the merged operation. Depending upon the definition of average administrative cost employed, merging appears to reduce costs by 20-25 percent. The fact that the merged organizational form is more efficient and less commonly observed further supports the notion that the Blues are not cost minimizers.

Chapter 4 contains the analysis of Medicare administrative costs. Because Medicare is administered by two entities, the federal government and the Carriers-Intermediaries, we have examined both sets of administrators. Furthermore, because Medicare has two parts, Part A, the hospital insurance plan, and Part B, the supplementary medical insurance plan, we have done a separate analysis of each part.

Government administration of Medicare ranges from investigations conducted by the Secret Service of the U.S. Treasury Department on the forgery of government checks to the large staff maintained by the Social Security

Administration, which performs such functions as data processing, operating district offices and reimbursing Carriers and Intermediaries. Analysis of the way costs are allocated between Part A and Part B and the way they are imputed to various parts of the operation in both a direct and indirect manner indicates that generally acceptable and sound accounting procedures are used. In fact, there is no reason to believe that there is any difference in the way Medicare's direct and indirect costs are imputed than the way a firm such as General Motors would impute costs between, say, its Frigidaire and Chevrolet Divisions.

Medicare accounts for a significant percentage of the Intermediaries' business. In 1971, the Intermediaries served 74.9 million people under their regular business and 20.4 million people, or 27 percent of their regular business under Medicare and, for many of the Intermediaries, Medicare benefits as a percentage of regular business benefits (claims costs) are quite substantial. In a large proportion of cases, they are over 100 percent.

Medicare also accounts for a significant percentage of the business of the Carriers. For the thirty-one Blue Shield plans which are Carriers under Medicare, Part B, Medicare enrollment coverage as a percent of regular coverage was 22.5 percent in fiscal 1971. Medicare benefit payments as a percentage of regular benefit payments amounted to 60.6 percent but there is a substantial variation among the plans. Of the thirteen commercial Intermediaries and Carriers for which data were available, only three companies had Medicare benefits which exceeded 50 percent of regular benefits in fiscal 1971 and all three companies were relatively small.

We examined two principal economic reasons why an insurer would want to become an Intermediary or Carrier under Medicare. The first reason has to do with economies of scale: if a firm can achieve greater economies in expanding its volume of business by taking on a Medicare clientele, then it will do so. The other reason is that a process which the Senate Finance Committee staff has described as "carving out" may be initiated:[2] because Medicare reimburses the Intermediaries and Carriers at cost for the administrative functions which they perform, the Intermediaries and Carriers have an incentive to maximize administrative costs rather than minimize them. Furthermore they can become more competitive in their regular business by allocating as much of their regular business administrative costs as possible onto Medicare administrative costs. More work needs to be done on this particular problem of perverse incentives but there is a large literature on the defense industry, where cost and cost-plus contracting were employed extensively in the past, which indicates that management does take the line of least resistance and yields to the incentive to maximize costs rather than minimize them.[b]

We attempted to estimate separate Medicare Part A and Part B cost functions with multivariate regression analysis. Given our theory of nonprofit firm behavior in Chapter 3 and given that Medicare provides an incentive to maximize

[b]This literature was documented in Chapter 4.

administrative costs, we did not expect to be able to estimate successful cost functions for the Intermediaries and Carriers. Our two principal dependent variables were Medicare administrative costs divided by Medicare benefit payments plus administrative costs (MOPCOST) and Medicare administrative costs divided by the number of bills paid (MUNCOST). The independent variables used were those related to firm size, bill type characteristics, and per capita income. We also tried using independent variables related to the Medicare clientele such as percentage over age sixty-five, percentage black, and percentage below the poverty level, independent variables related to provider characteristics such as average bed size of hospitals, percentage of hospitals which are teaching hospitals and state and local government hospitals, and variables related to the characteristics of the physician population. None of these independent variables explained variations in Medicare administrative costs very well.

One paradoxical finding in the Part A regression model is that, after having held all other variables constant, firm size is positively related to the level of administrative costs. There are at least two ways of interpreting the sign of the coefficient on the size variable. The first interpretation would imply that "carving out" does occur and that the larger Blue Cross intermediaries are more efficient at "carving out" than the smaller Blue Cross intermediaries. For this interpretation to be completely convincing, however, the coefficient on the size variable in the regular business equations in Chapter 3 would have had to be negative; that coefficient was not negative. One might still argue that "carving out" occurs under Medicare and that the larger Blue Cross plans still have higher costs than the smaller Blue Cross plans in their regular business because of more favorable treatment vis-à-vis their commercial competition. This argument is simply less convincing. The second interpretation of the positive sign of the size coefficient is that large intermediaries are less efficient than small intermediaries. This interpretation is difficult to accept because of findings of economies of scale in other studies of other parts of the insurance industry. Clearly, further research must be done on this issue. Finally, the Medicare Part B regression results indicate that the commercial carriers have lower operating costs than their Blue Shield counterparts.

Throughout the analysis, we have tried consciously not to make comparisons between the three insuring entities on the basis of cost ratios. While the cost ratio is useful for many analytic purposes, such as for running regression analysis on each separate group of insurers, it is not very useful for purposes of comparison. As we emphasized earlier, the types of service which each entity offers are so materially different that comparison of administrative cost ratios is akin to the proverbial comparison of apples and oranges. All three insuring entities offer pure health insurance protection, and then they offer a myriad of other services along with that pure protection. It would be comforting to know what a "basic" service package, over and above the insurance, "ought" to be and what it "ought" to cost. Then it would be possible to remove all of the fringe services from each insuring entity's package of services and compare the costs of all three ensuring entities "basic" service packages with each other, or with the costs of a model basic package determined by time-motion studies. Unfortunately, the sciences of economics and accounting have not yet reached that degree of analytical sophistication in dealing with the service industry.

Implications for National Health Insurance

The results of this study have some important implications for national health insurance. Many of the current proposals envision a system whereby standard health insurance packages will have to be provided to all employees. The employer will obviously want to minimize the costs of providing these packages. On efficiency grounds, then, our findings of economies of scale for commercial insurers indicate that national health insurance ought to be somewhat centralized in the hands of large, competitive firms. This is not to say that Blue Cross-Blue Shield has no role to play in the national health insurance program. Our findings on the Blues, however, do indicate that the artificial competitive advantages enjoyed by the Blues ought to be eliminated so that administrative slack will not impede the achievement of economies of scale in the competitive process.

The standardized insurance packages, which all the major bills on national health insurance require, will remove the current problem of consumer confusion with the plethora of policies now available. As market imperfections due to consumer befuddlement are reduced, price competition will become more important. There will be two beneficial results of the increasing importance of price competition. First, administrative costs will be held to a minimum. Second, although selling costs cannot be removed entirely, they will be held to the socially efficient level.

There are, however, several tempering factors. For one thing, if all existing insurers are of the minimum efficient size, the industry will be significantly more concentrated than it now is. With far fewer firms, collusive behavior is more likely. Of course, if the firms collude, then there is no reason to expect that society will enjoy the benefits of efficient administration. For another thing consumer confusion will not be totally eliminated by the standardized packages. There will always be room for supplemental insurance to complement or extend the mandatory coverage. We should not expect these policies to be any less confusing than those currently available. Finally, some members of the population, viz., the poor and elderly, will have their national health insurance purchased for them by the government.[c] If the government handles this the way Medicare is handled, we will have the insurance firms doing the administrative

[c]We assume that lump sums of cash will not be given to them to purchase their own insurance.

work and the government reimbursing them. If the insurers are reimbursed at cost, then the same perverse incentive to maximize, rather than minimize, administrative costs that exists under Medicare will be introduced into this segment of the national health insurance program. One way to avoid this perverse incentive is the payment of capitation administrative costs. Such a payment scheme would restore the incentive to minimize costs. The appropriate capitation rate could be determined through an iterative process.

Efficiency in administration, however, may not be the sole criterion for the choice of the form of national health insurance administration. Given the rapid increase in the cost of medical care and the exacerbating influence of national health insurance, we may wish to establish a system that will hold down the costs of medical services. There are two distinct roles that an insurer can play in the payment process. First, there is the *conduit* role. When the insurance firm assumes this role, it merely pays the bills that are submitted. The consumer faces several price variables in the medical care market: the annual health insurance premium, the deductible on his policy, and the coinsurance on bills above the deductible. Even when the insurer assumes the conduit role, the individual consumer exercises indirect control over the cost of a given quality of medical services through his willingness to pay premiums, deductibles, and coinsurance. An alternative role for the insurer to assume is that of an *advocate*. Assumption of this role by the insurer amounts to explicit recognition of the fact that the insurer enjoys more market power than the individual consumer and thereby has more ability to control the cost of a given quality of health care. In fact, given the nature of the insurance transaction and the manner in which bills are paid, the insurer really becomes a surrogate buyer of medical services. Consequently, one may expect the insurer to assume some responsibility for controlling the consumer's cost of a given quality of care.

Feldstein has shown that the *conduit* concept of administration plus first dollar insurance leads inexorably to inflation in the health sector. The inevitability of inflation results from the lack of a nexus between the payment for a medical service and the consumption of it. First dollar insurance creates permanent excess demand for health services.[3] Because there is no direct link between what providers charge and what consumers are really willing to pay, there are no competitive pressures on providers to hold down costs. Consequently, prices in the medical care sector have risen at much more rapid rates than in other sectors of the economy. This has been particularly true as insurance coverage has broadened and deepened through the advent of Medicare and Medicaid.[4]

If one of the major subsidiary concerns of the national health insurance program is to mitigate the spiraling prices in the medical care industry, administration by large competing firms may not be a practical way to attain this objective. In the presently atomized health insurance industry, there is no evidence that the advocacy role is now being exercised. To the extent that consumer confusion is reduced by standardization of coverage, competitive forces should be expected to result in a more concentrated market structure.

Nonetheless, the industry will support a substantial number of firms of minimum, efficient size. This will yield a market structure that is still insufficiently concentrated to support an advocacy role for the remaining firms. Given competitive pressures, no single firm will have an incentive to try to hold down prices.

A priori reasoning suggests that the advocacy role could be better exercised by a monopsonistic buyer of health care. Unfortunately, there is a disturbing trade off to be made. Although one cannot be sure whether present Medicare administrative costs are high or low, the presumption is that they are higher than they would be if Medicare were administered under a competitive system. Medicare is a monopsonistic buyer of health care for some 10 percent of the population. If the Social Security Administration or another similar agency were to become the sole administrator for the entire population, then we should expect national health insurance to be administered less efficiently than under a conduit role competitive situation. In contrast, the savings in benefit payments by having a monopsonistic advocate could more than offset the possibly increased administrative costs, which could result from a lack of competition. There is a third option that would preserve the competitive aspect plus the advocacy role. National health insurance payments could be made to insurers or health maintenance organizations on a capitation basis rather than on a premium basis. Use of an iterative procedure could determine the capitation fee. This type of payment would serve to internalize the incentives for efficiency just as it has done in presently existing health maintenance organizations. Insurers, thus, would have strong internal incentives to assume an advocacy role.

Notes

1. For a more general discussion of the infrequency of homogeneous outputs, see G.J. Stigler, "A Theory of Oligopoly," *Journal of Political Economy* 72 (February 1964):44-61.

2. Staff Report, Senate Finance Committee, *Medicare and Medicaid: Problems, Issues, and Alternatives* (Washington: U.S. Government Printing Office, February 9, 1970), p. 116.

3. Martin S. Feldstein, "The Rising Price of Physicians' Services," *Review of Economics and Statistics*, May 1970, p. 132, and *The Rising Cost of Hospital Care* (Washington: Information Resources Press, 1971).

4. Ibid. Feldstein eloquently documents these increases and explains their causality.

Appendixes

Appendix A

Instructions to BHI Analyst for Preparation of HI/SMI Split

In Chapter 4, we analyzed the administrative costs of the Medicare program. One of the administrative decisions that must necessarily be made is how to divide Medicare administrative costs between Part A hospital insurance (HI) and Part B supplementary medical insurance (SMI). We noted in Chapter 4 that generally sound accounting procedures were used and that internal competition would insure a proper allocation of costs. This Appendix contains the accounting rules which were established by the Bureau of Health Insurance of the Social Security Administration for the allocation of costs between HI and SMI. We include this material so that the interested reader might trace out for himself the procedure actually followed by BHI cost accountants.

Instructions

Obtain the distribution of Activity 3 costs between HI and SMI for fiscal years 19PY, 19CY, and 19BY from the BDOO, BRSI, BDPA, BHA, and ORS analysts (instructions for making the distribution are given in Part 14 of the Budget Mechanization Instructions Manual).

For each of the three fiscal years, prepare the overall HI/SMI split according to the following (the item titles will correspond to those used on the worksheet):

ITEM	EXPLANATION
A. Identifiable Costs	Workloads and other cost items which can be specifically identified with either HI or SMI—show MYs and total money (numbers from analysts' submissions) for BDOO, BRSI, BHI, BDPA, ORS, and BHA.
Sub-Total A	Total Identifiable Costs.
B. Common Costs	Show MYs and total money for BDOO, BRSI, BHI (showing separate figures for "Intermediaries" and "States"), BDPA and ORS as distributed by respective analysts in their submissions.

ITEM	EXPLANATION
Sub-Total B	Total Common Costs.
Total A and B	Total Identifiable and Common Costs.
% Manpower	Show percentage HI-MYs and SMI-MYs each represent of total MYs shown in the item above.
OPEP, OC, OCF, OACT, OA, OPA, CCE (Orig. Act. 3 Split per above percentage)	Original Act. 3 totals for both HI and SMI less "Total A and B" items combined for HI and SMI. The remainder, representing that portion of Act. 3 not yet split, should be split between HI and SMI according to the MY percentages calculated for the item above.
Sub-Total (Controls to Orig. Act. 3 Total)	Here, HI sub-total plus SMI sub-total should equal original Act. 3 total for both HI and SMI.
Act. 4 (Amount prorated to Act. 3)	1. Obtain the following Act. 4 data from the BDPA analyst (*sample* figures are included here to make these instructions easier to follow):

a. A/N Maintenance Function
   Percentage related to HI—10%
   Percentage related to SMI—4%

b. E/R Maintenance Function
   Percentage related to HI—12%
   (Since insured status is not a factor for SMI enrollment, there are no E/R maintenance costs distributed to SMI).

c. Split between A/N and E/R of total Act. 4. MYs to be distributed to Act. 3.

	A/N	E/R	Total
HI	200 MY	400 MY	600 MY
SMI	40 MY	0	40 MY
Total	240 MY	400 MY	640 MY

ITEM	EXPLANATION
	2. From data in step 1,C. above, determine the percent of total Act. 4 MYs to be distributed to Act. 3 which are related to *A/N* maintenance function and the percent related to *E/R* maintenance function: $$A/N = \frac{240}{640} = 37.5\%$$ 3. Determine value for HI and SMI portions weighted for the proportions of *A/N* work and *E/R* work: HI: 10% (*A/N* maintenance) x 37.5% = .0375 12% (*E/R* maintenance) x 62.5% = .0750 .1125 SMI: 4% (*A/N* maintenance) x 37.5% = .0150 4. Determine from weighted values deived in step 3 the relative HI/SMI percentage of total: HI – .1125) rounded 88.2% SMI – .0150) 11.8% .1275 100.0% 5. Use these percentages to split Act. 4 MYs and money to be distributed to Act. 3 between HI and SMI.
Grand Total	
C.1 Total Identified Uninsured	Sum of items shown (with asterisks) by analysts in their submissions to be solely attributable to HI uninsured beneficiaries.
C.2 Balance HI Costs	Grand Total above less item C.1.
Grand Total HI Insured	Grand Total above less Grand Total of HI Uninsured (see below).
Grand Total HI Uninsured	1. Subtract "Total Identified Uninsured" MYs and money from "Subtotal" (controls to Orig. Act.

ITEM	EXPLANATION

3)—this is to avoid double-counting of identified uninsured costs.

2. To split Act. 3 between HI insured and uninsured, prorate the figures derived in Step 1 above according to the percentage split of total HI benefit payments between insured and uninsured. (HI benefit payment data is provided by OAct.)

3. To split Act. 4 distributed to HI between insured and uninsured, it is necessary to refer back to some of the data used in deriving the HI/SMI Act. 4 split (the same sample figures will be used for this calculation). Since *E/R* maintenance is not a workload applicable to the HI uninsured, the portion of Act. 4 prorated to Act. 3 which represents *E/R* maintenance should not be applied to HI uninsured. Using the previous sample figures, the weighted value for the HI portion of the Act. 4 distribution is *.1125*, composed of:

.0375 (*A/N* maintenance)	or	33.3%
.0750 (*E/R* maintenance)		66.7%
		100.0%

In this example, since 66.7% of the total is associated with *E/R* maintenance, only 33.3% of the HI portion of Act. 4 prorated to Act. 3 should be split between insured and uninsured, using the percentage splits of total HI benefit payments between insured and uninsured (also used in Step 2 above).

EXPLANATION

4. For both man-years and money, total the uninsured portions obtained in Steps 2 and 3 above. Then, add the "Total Identified Uninsured" back in. The result represents "Grand Total Uninsured."

Appendix B: Intermediaries and Carriers Used in Regressions

Chapter 4 contains the separate regression analysis of the administrative costs of the Medicare Part A Intermediaries and the Part B Carriers. This Appendix lists those Intermediaries and Carriers that were the units of observation in the regressions.

Part A–Intermediaries

1. Aetna–Hartford, Connecticut
2. Memphis Hospital Service & Surgical Association
3. Connecticut Blue Cross (B.C.)
4. Utah B.C.
5. Indiana B.C.
6. Associated Hospital Service of Maine
7. Massachusetts Hospital Service
8. Aetna–Worcester, Massachusetts
9. New Hampshire-Vermont Hospitalization Service
10. Hospital Service Corporation of Rhode Island
11. Hospital Service Plan of New Jersey
12. Prudential-Millville, New Jersey
13. Blue Cross of Northeastern New York, Inc.
14. Blue Cross of Western New York, Inc.
15. Chautauqua Region Hospital Service Corporation
16. Associated Hospital Service of New York
17. Rochester Hospital Service Corporation
18. Rochester Hospital Service Corporation
19. Group Hospital Service, Inc., Syracuse
20. Hospital Plan, Incorporated, Utica
21. Hospital Service Corporation of Jefferson County, Watertown
22. Blue Cross of Puerto Rico
23. Blue Cross-Blue Shield of Delaware
24. Maryland Hospital Service, Inc.
25. Inter-County Hospitalization Plan, Inc., Glenside, Pennsylvania
26. Blue Cross of Lehigh Valley, Allentown, Pennsylvania
27. Capital Blue Cross, Harrisburg, Pennsylvania
28. Blue Cross of Greater Philadelphia
29. Blue Cross of Western Pennsylvania, Pittsburgh
30. Blue Cross of Northerneastern Pennsylvania, Wilkes-Barre

31. Virginia Hospital Service Association, Richmond
32. Hospital Service Association of Roanoke
33. Blue Cross Hospital Service, Inc., Charleston, West Virginia
34. Parkersburg Hospital Service, Inc., West Virginia
35. West Virginia Hospital Service, Inc., Wheeling
36. Hospital Service Association of New Orleans
37. Blue Cross-Blue Shield of Alabama
38. Blue Cross of Florida, Inc., Jacksonville
39. United Hospitals Service Association, Atlanta
40. Georgia Hospital Service Association, Columbus
41. Blue Cross Hospital Plan, Inc., Louisville, Kentucky
42. Mississippi Hospital and Medical Service, Jackson
43. The Blue Cross Plans of North Carolina, Chapel Hill
44. South Carolina Hospital Service Plan, Columbia
45. Tennessee Hospital Service Association, Chattanooga
46. Chicago B.C.
47. Illinois Hospital and Health Service, Inc., Rockford
48. Michigan Hospital Service, Detroit
49. Hospital Service, Inc., Albuquerque
50. Blue Cross Hospital Plan, Inc., Canton, Ohio
51. Hospital Care Corporation, Cincinnati
52. Blue Cross of Northeast Ohio, Cleveland
53. Blue Cross of Central Ohio, Columbus
54. Hospital Service, Inc., Lima, Ohio
55. Blue Cross of Northwest Ohio, Toledo
56. Associated Hospital Service, Inc., Youngstown
57. Associated Hospital Service, Inc., Milwaukee
58. Arkansas Blue Cross and Blue Shield, Inc., Little Rock
59. Louisiana Hospital Service, Baton Rouge
60. New Mexico B.C.
61. Group Hospital Service, Tulsa
62. Group Hospital Service, Inc., Dallas
63. Hospital Service, Inc., Des Moines, Iowa
64. Associated Hospitals Service, Sioux City, Iowa
65. Group Hospital Service, Inc., Kansas City
66. Kansas Hospital Service Association, Inc., Topeka
67. Blue Cross Hospital Service, Inc. of Missouri, St. Louis
68. Nebraska Blue Cross Hospital Service Association, Omaha
69. Colorado Hospital Service, Denver
70. Blue Cross of Montana
71. Blue Cross of North Dakota
72. Wyoming Hospital Service, Cheyenne
73. Associated Hospital Service of Arizona, Phoenix

74. Kaiser Foundation Health Plan, Inc., Oakland
75. Hospital Service of Southern California, Los Angeles
76. Hospital Service of California, Oakland
77. Hawaii Medical Service Association
78. California–Kaiser
79. Aetna Life and Casualty, Reno
80. Washington Hospital Service Association, Seattle
81. Idaho Hospital Service
82. Northwest Hospital Service, Portland
83. Hawaii–Kaiser
84. Aetna Life & Casualty, Seattle
85. Travelers, Hartford
86. Travelers, Lowell, Massachusetts
87. Travelers, Garden City, New York
88. Travelers, Pittsburgh
89. Aetna Life and Casualty, Clearwater, Florida
90. Travelers, Atlanta
91. Aetna Life and Casualty, Peoria, Illinois
92. Memphis–Aetna
93. Travelers, Detroit
94. Travelers, Rochester, Minnesota
95. Nationwide, Columbus, Ohio
96. Aetna Life and Casualty, Los Angeles
97. Travelers, Los Angeles
98. Mutual of Omaha, Omaha

Part B–Carriers

1. Connecticut General
2. Union Mutual
3. Massachusetts Blue Shield (B.S.)
4. New Hampshire-Vermont B.S.
5. Rhode Island B.S.
6. Delaware B.S.
7. Prudential–New Jersey
8. New York Group Health
9. Metropolitan–New York
10. Buffalo, New York B.S.
11. New York, New York B.S.
12. Rochester, New York B.S.
13. District of Columbia B.S.
14. Metropolitan–Kentucky

15. Maryland B.S.
16. Pennsylvania B.S.
17. Puerto Rico B.S.
18. Travelers–Virginia
19. Nationwide
20. Alabama B.S.
21. Florida B.S.
22. Travelers–Mississippi
23. South Carolina B.S.
24. Equitable–Tennessee
25. Prudential–North Carolina
26. Illinois B.S.
27. Continental–Illinois
28. Indiana B.S.
29. Michigan B.S.
30. Ohio B.S.
31. Nationwide–Ohio
32. Madison, Wisconsin B.S.
33. Milwaukee, Wisconsin B.S.
34. Iowa B.S.
35. Kansas B.S.
36. Missouri B.S.
37. Minnesota B.S.
38. Travelers–Minnesota
39. General American–Missouri
40. Mutual of Omaha–Nebraska
41. North Dakota B.S.
42. South Dakota B.S.
43. Arkansas B.S.
44. Pan American–Louisiana
45. Equitable–New Mexico
46. Aetna–Oklahoma
47. Dept. of Welfare–Oklahoma
48. Texas B.S.
49. Colorado B.S.
50. Equitable–Idaho
51. Montana B S.
52. Utah B.S.
53. Equitable–Wyoming
54. Aetna–Oregon
55. Aetna–Arizona
56. California B.S.
57. Occidental–California

58. Aetna–Hawaii
59. Aetna–Nevada
60. Chelan, Washington B.S.
61. Pierce, Washington B.S.
62. Snohomish, Washington B.S.
63. Yakima, Washington B.S.
64. King, Washington B.S.
65. Spokane, Washington B.S.

Bibliography

Bibliography

Arrow, Kenneth J. "Uncertainty and the Welfare Economics of Medical Care." *American Economic Review* 53, 5 (December 1963).

Arrow, Kenneth J. *Social Choice and Individual Values.* New Haven: Yale University Press, 1951.

Belth, Joseph M. "Statement on Price Competition in the Life Insurance Market." Subcommittee on Antitrust and Monopoly of the U.S. Senate Committee on the Judiciary, February 1973.

Blair, Roger D.; Jackson, Jerry; and Vogel, Ronald J. "Economies of Scale in the Administration of Health Insurance." *Review of Economics and Statistics* 57 (May 1975).

Blair, Roger D.; Ginsburg, Paul; and Vogel, Ronald J. "Blue Cross-Blue Shield Administrative Costs: A Study of Non-Profit Health Insurers." *Economic Inquiry* 13 (June 1975).

Blue Cross-Blue Shield Association. *Blue Cross and Blue Shield Fact Book 1972.* Chicago: Blue Cross Association and National Association of Blue Shield Plans, 1972.

Blue Cross Association. *Blue Cross Comparative Cost Report on the 1971 National Cost Report.* Chicago: Blue Cross Association, 1972.

Comptroller General of the United States, General Accounting Office. *Acquisition of Major Weapon Systems*, March 18, 1971.

Cooper, Barbara S. and Worthington, Nancy L. "Age Differences in Medical Care Spending–Fiscal Year 1972." *Social Security Bulletin*, May 1973.

Cooper, Barbara S. and Worthington, Nancy L. "Medical Care Outlays for Three Age Groups." *Social Security Bulletin*, May 1971.

Cyert, R.M. and March, J.G. *A Behavioral Theory of the Firm.* Englewood Cliffs: Prentice-Hall, 1963.

Davis, Karen. "Theories of Hospital Inflation: Some Empirical Evidence." *Journal of Human Resources*, Spring 1973.

Denenberg, Herbert S. "Statement," before the Antitrust and Monopoly Subcommittee of the U.S. Senate Committee on the Judiciary, May 11, 1972.

Eilers, Robert D. "National Health Insurance: What Kind and How Much." *New England Journal of Medicine*, April 1971.

Eilers, Robert D. and Moyerman, Sue (eds.). *Proceedings of the Conference on National Health Insurance.* Homewood: Richard D. Irwin, Inc., 1971.

Feldstein, Martin S. "An Econometric Model of the Medicare System: Reply." *Quarterly Journal of Economics*, August 1973.

Feldstein, Martin S. "The Welfare Loss of Excess Health Insurance." *Journal of Political Economy*, March/April 1973.

Feldstein, Martin S. "An Econometric Model of the Medicare System." *Quarterly Journal of Economics*, February 1971.

Feldstein, Martin S. *The Rising Cost of Hospital Care.* Washington: Information Resources Press, 1971.

Feldstein, Martin S. "Hospital Cost Inflation: A Study of Non-Profit Price Dynamics." *American Economic Review*, December 1971.

Feldstein, Martin S. "The Rising Price of Physicians' Services." *Review of Economics and Statistics*, May 1970.

Fuchs, Victor, R. "The Basic Forces Influencing the Costs of Medical Care." In National Conference on Medical Costs, Washington, D.C., June 27-28, 1967, *Report.* Washington: U.S. Government Printing Office, 1967.

Ginsburg, Paul B. "Capital Investment by Non-Profit Firms: The Voluntary Hospital." Michigan State University Econometrics Workshop Paper 7205, revised June 1973.

Ginsburg, Paul B., and Allen, B.J. "Statistical Analysis of Hospital Mergers." Paper presented to the Econometric Society December 27-30, 1973.

Health Insurance Institute. *1972-73 Source Book of Health Insurance Data.* New York: Health Insurance Institute, 1973.

Hensley, Roy J. "Economics of Scale in Financial Enterprises." *Journal of Political Economy*, October 1958.

Hensley, Roy J. *Competition, Regulation and the Public Interest in Nonlife Insurance.* Berkeley: University of California Press, 1962.

Houston, David B. and Simon, Richard M. "Economies of Scale in Financial Institutions: A Study in Life Insurance." *Econometrica* 38, 6 (November 1970).

Johnston, J. *Econometric Methods*, 2nd ed. New York: McGraw-Hill, 1972.

Kmenta, Jan. *Elements of Econometrics.* New York: The Macmillan Company, 1971.

Krizay, John and Wilson, Andrew. *The Patient as Consumer: Health Care Financing in the United States.* Lexington: D.C. Heath and Company, 1974.

Krizay, John F. "Health Insurance: Can the Government Do It Cheaper?" *Bests Review*, January 1973.

Krizay, John F. "Does the Social Security Administration Really Run Medicare on Two Percent of Income?" *Perspective*, Fourth Quarter, 1972.

Lancaster, Kelvin. "Change and Innovation in the Technology of Consumption." *American Economic Review*, May 1966.

Lancaster, Kelvin. "A New Approach to Consumer Theory." *Journal of Political Economy*, April 1966.

Law, Sylvia A. *Blue Cross What Went Wrong?* New Haven: Yale University Press, 1974.

Lave, Judith R. and Lave, Lester B. "Hospital Cost Functions." *American Economic Review*, June 1970.

Lee, M.L. "A Conspicuous Production Theory of Hospital Behavior." *Southern Economic Journal*, July 1971.

MacIntyre, Duncan M. *Voluntary Health Insurance and Rate Making.* Ithaca: Cornell University Press, 1962.

Moore, Frederick F. *Military Procurement and Contracting: An Economic Analysis.* RAND Corporation, R.M.-2948-P.R., 1962.

Mueller, Marjorie Smith. "Private Health Insurance in 1971: Health Care Services, Enrollment, and Finances." *Social Security Bulletin*, February 1973.

National Underwriter Company. *1972 Argus Chart of Health Insurance.* Cincinnati: National Underwriter, 1972.

National Underwriter Company. *Time Saver.* Cincinnati: The National Underwriter Company, 1972.

National Association of Blue Shield Plans. *1971 National Cost Report Statistical Summary.* Chicago: National Association of Blue Shield B Plans, 1972.

Newhouse, Joseph. "Toward a Theory of Non-Profit Institutions: An Economic Model of a Hospital." *American Economic Review*, March 1970.

Owens, Arthur. "Time Well Spent?: New Norms Will Help You See." *Medical Economics*, December 6, 1971.

Pauly, Mark V. and Redisch, Michael. "The Hospital as a Physicians' Cooperative." *American Economic Review*, March 1973.

Pauly, Mark V. "The Economics of Moral Hazard." *American Economic Review*, June 1968.

Peck, M.J. and Scherer, F.M. *The Weapons Acquisition Process: An Economic Analysis.* Cambridge: Harvard University Press, 1962.

Perry, Robert, et al. *System Acquisition Strategies.* R.-733-PR/ARPA, RAND Corporation, June 1971.

Phelps, Charles E. *Demand for Health Insurance: A Theoretical and Empirical Investigation.* RAND Corporation, R-1054-OEO, July 1973.

Reed, Louis S. *Financial Experiences of Health Insurance Organizations in the United States.* Social Security Administration, Office of Research and Statistics, Research Report No. 12, 1965.

Russell, Louise B. "An Econometric Model of the Medicare System: Comment." *Quarterly Journal of Economics*, August 1973.

Scherer, Frederick M. "The Aerospace Industry." In Walter Adams (ed.), *The Structure of American Industry*. New York: The Macmillan Company, 1971.

Scherer, Frederick M. *The Weapons Acquisition Process: Economic Incentives.* Cambridge: Harvard University Press, 1964.

Schuchardt, Robert A. *Managerial Accounting in the Property and Casualty Business.* Cincinnati: The National Underwriter Company, 1969.

Somers, Herman M. and Somers, Anne R. *Doctors, Patients and Health Insurance.* Washington: The Brookings Institution, 1961.

Stigler, George J. "A Theory of Oligopoly." *Journal of Political Economy* 72 (February 1964).

U.S. Congress, Joint Economic Committee, Subcommittee on Priorities and Economy in Government. *The Acquisition of Weapons Systems.* Part 7, November 14, 15 and 16, 1973.

U.S. Department of Commerce. *Survey of Current Business,* December, 1972.

U.S. Department of Health, Education and Welfare, Social Security Administration, Bureau of Health Insurance. *Analysis of Intermediaries' and Carriers' Administrative Costs*, July-June 1972 and July-June 1971.

U.S. Department of Health, Education and Welfare, National Center for Health Statistics. *Age Patterns in Medical Care, Illness and Disability–United States*, July 1963-June 1965.

U.S. Department of Health, Education and Welfare, Social Security Administration. *Health Insurance for the Aged, Part I, Administration, Part B., Intermediary Manual*, HIM 14-1 (8-67), Reprint Date (4-72).

U.S. Department of Health, Education and Welfare, Advisory Committee on Medicare Administration, Contracting and Subcontracting. *Report to the Secretary of HEW and the Commissioner of Social Security*, June 21, 1974, HEW publication MAGS-2 (6-74).

U.S. Department of Health, Education and Welfare, Social Security Administration. *Private Health Insurance and Medical Care: Conference Papers.* Washington: U.S. Government Printing Office, 1968.

U.S. Department of Labor, Bureau of Labor Statistics. *Handbook of Labor Statistics*, 1972. Washington: U.S. Government Printing Office, 1972.

U.S. House Committee on Ways and Means. *Analysis of Health Insurance Proposals Introduced in the 92nd Congress.* Washington: U.S. Government Printing Office, 1971.

U.S. House of Representatives, Committee on Ways and Means. *Basic Facts on the Health Industry*, 92nd Congress, 1st Session. Washington: U.S. Government Printing Office, 1971.

U.S. Senate Finance Committee, Staff Report. *Medicare and Medicaid: Problems, Issues and Alternatives.* Washington: U.S. Government Printing Office, February 9, 1970.

Vogel, Ronald J. "Trends in Health Insurance Operating Expenses: Comment." *New England Journal of Medicine*, January 1973.

Vogel, Ronald J. and Blair, Roger D. "An Analysis of Medicare Administrative Costs." *Social Security Bulletin* 37 (August 1974):3-23.

Waldman, Saul. *National Health Insurance Proposals: Provisions of Bills Introduced in the 93rd Congress as of October 1973.* Social Administration, Office of Research and Statistics, DHEW publication No. SSA-74-11916.

Weiss, R.J. et al. "Trends in Health Insurance Operating Expenses." *New England Journal of Medicine*, September 1972.

Williamson, Oliver F. *The Economics of Discretionary Behavior: Managerial Objectives in a Theory of the Firm.* Englewood Cliffs: Prentice-Hall, 1964.

Woodcock, Leonard. "Statement" before the Subcommittee on Antitrust and Monopoly of the U.S. Senate Committee on the Judiciary, May 11, 1972.

Index

Index

About the Authors

Roger D. Blair received the Ph.D. from Michigan State University in 1968. Following military service, he joined the faculty in the Department of Economics at the University of Florida where he is currently an associate professor. Dr. Blair has contributed to the *Review of Economics and Statistics, Economic Inquiry, Land Economics* and the *Antitrust Law and Economics Review.*

Ronald J. Vogel received the Ph.D. in economics from the University of Wisconsin in 1967. Since then, he has taught at both Cornell University and the University of Florida. During the academic year 1971-72, he served as Brookings Institution Economic Policy Fellow in the Office of the Secretary, Department of Health, Education and Welfare. From 1972 to 1975 he was a Research Economist in the Office of Research and Statistics, Social Security Administration and currently he is a staff economist at the Urban Institute. His present research interests are in the areas of health economics and public finance.

Related Lexington Books

Association of Life Insurance Medical Directors and Society of Actuaries, *Medical Risks: Patterns of Mortality and Survival*, In Press.

Bailey, Elizabeth E. *Economic Theory of Regulatory Constraint*, 224 pp., 1973

Cummins, J. David, *An Econometric Model of the Life Insurance Sector of the U.S. Economy,* 272 pp, 1975

Hohahan, John, *Financing Health Care for the Poor: The Medicaid Experience*, 176 pp., 1975

Keintz, Rita M. *National Health Insurance and Income Distribution*, In Press.

Krizay, John and Wilson, Andrew A., *The Patient as Consumer: Health Care Financing in the United States*, 256 pp., 1974